Academic Learning Series

Microsoft®
Windows NT® Network Administration

Lab Manual

Microsoft Press

PUBLISHED BY
Microsoft Press
A Division of Microsoft Corporation
One Microsoft Way
Redmond, Washington 98052-6399

Library of Congress Cataloging-in-Publication Data
Microsoft Windows NT Network Administration: Academic Learning Series /
Microsoft Corporation
p. cm.
Includes index.
ISBN 1-57231-439-7
ISBN 1-57231-913-5 (Academic Learning Series)
1. Microsoft Windows NT. 2. Operating systems (Computers) I. Microsoft Corporation.
QA76.76.063M74516 1998
005.4'4769--dc21 97-52817
CIP

Printed and bound in the United States of America.

6 7 8 9 WCWC 3 2 1 0 9

Distributed in Canada by Penguin Books Canada Limited.

A CIP catalogue record for this book is available from the British Library.

Microsoft Press books are available through booksellers and distributors worldwide. For further information about international editions, contact your local Microsoft Corporation office, or contact Microsoft Press International directly at fax (425) 936-7329. Visit our Web site at mspress.microsoft.com.

Acquisitions Editor: William Setten
Series Editor: Barbara Moreland

Part No. 097-0002057

Introduction to Lab Exercises

Included with the Academic Learning Series (ALS) texts are hands-on lab exercises designed to give you practical experience using Microsoft Windows NT 4.0. This hands-on experience is an essential part of your training because it is difficult to truly understand and use the operating system and its features without having had the opportunity to explore firsthand the menus, options, and responses. The tasks included in these exercises provide an opportunity for you to test the concepts presented in the text, to use Microsoft Windows NT's utilities and tools, and to explore the structure of Microsoft Windows NT's operating system.

The lab exercises are best used in a classroom setting, though some exercises can be completed individually. The exercises presume a classroom network setup in one or more Windows NT domains with shared resources (depending upon the specific ALS text being used).

The directory of subdirectories, programs, and data files designed to support these labs can be shared from the instructor's system or installed on each student's system. A lab setup guide is provided for the instructor to use in setting up the classroom to support the labs.

The lab exercises do not precisely mirror the text's practice activities. Domain names, user names, IP addresses, shared resources, and other specific references in the lab exercises may be somewhat different from similar references in the ALS text or from those used in setting up the classroom network.

Local constraints must be followed to ensure proper network operations. Since it is not possible to predict each institution's local networking requirements, your instructor will explain differences that occur.

The old saying "The way to get to Carnegie Hall is to practice, practice, practice" is equally true of the pursuit of personal competency and Microsoft Certification. The tests required for Microsoft Certified Product Specialist, Systems Engineer, or other Microsoft certifications are demanding. One of the best ways to become confident in the use of Microsoft Windows NT is to complete each of the assigned lab exercises as well as the practice tasks included in the text.

Note Worksheets required for exercises and labs are available on the CD-ROM that accompanies this book under the name "Planning Worksheets." You may print these documents and complete them by hand or work with them online.

Lab 1: Planning and Creating User Accounts

Objectives

After completing this lab, you will be able to:

- Plan how to implement new user accounts.
- Create user accounts.
- Create home folders for user accounts.
- Set logon hours restrictions.
- Set workstation restrictions.
- Set account restrictions.

Estimated time to complete this lab: 30 minutes

Exercise 1
Planning New User Accounts

In this exercise, you will work with a partner to plan how to implement user accounts for the employees of World Wide Importers. You and your partner will decide the names of the employees and record them on the *User and Group Accounts Planning Worksheet*. It is important that you complete this exercise, because the user accounts you create will be used throughout this course.

Scenario

As the Microsoft Windows NT administrator for World Wide Importers, you need to set up the user accounts for their Quebec office. You need to determine:

- A naming convention that will easily accommodate employees with duplicate or similar names, and temporary contract personnel.
- Who determines the password for an account.
- User logon hours and computer use.
- Whether home folders will be located on the local computer or a server.

Use the following criteria to make your decisions:

- Temporary contract employees should be able to log on to *only* their assigned computers and only from 8 A.M. to 5 P.M. Their computer names are \\Temp1 and \\Temp2.
- World Wide Importers hires approximately 300 new employees a year. Approximately 20 of those employees are hired on a one-year contract basis. All employees require a user account.
- The vice president's name is Susan Young, and the customer service representative who works the night shift is also named Susan Young.
- Passwords for permanent employees should be known only to the employee.
- For security reasons, passwords for contract employees should be controlled by the administrator.
- Each employee requires a secure home folder. All home folders need to be backed up each night.
- The day shift works from 8 A.M. to 5 P.M. The night shift works from 6 P.M. to 6 A.M.
- Employees who work the night shift should only be able to access the network from 6 P.M. to 6 A.M. All other permanent employees require access to the network 24 hours a day, 7 days a week.

To complete the *User and Group Accounts Planning Worksheet*, you and your partner need to:

1. Provide each user's full name, except where specified in the scenario. The Description column in the *User and Group Accounts Planning Worksheet* identifies the job title for each employee.
2. Determine each user name based on your naming convention.
3. Enter the password requirements, home folder location, logon hours, and workstation restrictions based on the criteria in the scenario.

Exercise 2
Creating User Accounts

In this exercise, you will work with your partner to create the user accounts from your *User and Group Accounts Planning Worksheet.*

This exercise is structured so that you first create all the accounts and then modify the properties of each account. If you have multiple accounts that require the same properties you can use the **Copy** command on the **User** menu to create a user account from an existing account.

Important The user accounts that you create must be unique to your domain's directory database. Because you and your partner are working in the same domain, you need to divide the accounts between you. One person should create the first half of the user accounts on the BDC, and the other person should create the second half of the user accounts on the PDC. Otherwise, only one of you can do the exercise.

➤ **To create a new user account**

1. Log on to your domain (DOMAIN*x*, where *x* is the number assigned to your domain) as Administrator.
2. Click **Start**, point to **Programs**, point to **Administrative Tools**, and then click **User Manager for Domains**.
3. On the **User** menu, click **New User**.

   The **New User** dialog box appears.
4. Configure the following options based on the information from the *User and Group Accounts Planning Worksheet.*
   - **Username**
   - **Full Name**
   - **Description**
   - **Password** (Use the word **password**. Passwords are case-sensitive.)
   - **Confirm Password**
5. Select the appropriate password options, and then click **Add**.

   The **New User** dialog box reappears and is cleared so that you can add another user.
6. Create the remaining user accounts.

7. When you have created all the accounts on your *User and Group Accounts Planning Worksheet*, close the **New User** dialog box to return to the User Manager window.

➤ To create a home folder

Note Complete this procedure for each user account.

1. In the User Manager window, double-click a user account.
2. In the **User Properties** dialog box, click **Profile**.
3. In the **Connect** box, click **Z:** so that drive Z will be used to connect to the user's home folder.
4. In the **To** box, type **\\student*x*\users\%username%** (where **student*x*** is the name of the PDC for your domain).

Note In the classroom setup, the \Users folder was created and shared on an NTFS volume on the PDC. In an actual working situation, you would also need to create and share a folder on an NTFS volume for this procedure to work.

5. Click **OK** to return to the **User Properties** dialog box.
6. Click **OK** to return to the User Manager window.

Tip To assign home folders to multiple accounts at one time using the %username% variable, in the User Manager window, select all accounts by pressing the CTRL key while you click each account. Then, on the **User** menu, click **Properties** to open the **User Properties** dialog box.

➤ To set logon hours restrictions

Note Complete this procedure for each user who requires logon restrictions.

1. In the **User Properties** dialog box, click **Hours**.

   Notice that the default is to allow the user to log on to the network 24 hours a day, 7 days a week.
2. To restrict a user's logon hours, select the appropriate block of time, and then click **Disallow**.

   For more information about using the **Logon Hours** box, click **Help**.
3. Click **OK**.

➤ To set workstation restrictions

Note Complete this procedure for each user who requires logon restrictions.

1. In the **User Properties** dialog box, click **Logon To**.

   Notice that the default is to allow a user to log on to all computers.
2. Click **User May Log On To These Workstations**.
3. In box 1, type the name of your computer (**student***x*, where *x* is your student number).
4. Click **OK**.

➤ To set the account restriction

Note Complete this procedure for each user whose account needs to expire.

1. In the **User Properties** dialog box, click **Account**.

   Notice that the default option for **Account Expires** is **Never**. The default **Account Type** is **Global Account**.
2. Click **End of**, and then type the appropriate date.
3. Click **OK**.

➤ To grant dial-in permission

Note From the PDC, grant the dial-in permission for the Accounting Manager. From the BDC, grant the dial-in permission for the Vice President.

1. In the **User Properties** dialog box, click **Dialin**.
2. Click Grant dialin permission to user.
3. Click **OK**.
4. Click **Add**.

Exercise 3
Testing the New User Accounts

In this exercise, you will work with your partner to test the user accounts that you just created.

➤ To determine that home folders were created

Note Complete this procedure from the PDC.

---

1. Start Windows NT Explorer and expand drive D.
2. Expand the D:\Winnt\Users folder.
3. Compare the folders in D:\Winnt\Users with the list of user names on your *User and Group Accounts Planning Worksheet.*

   Are there any differences? ____________________

   ____

4. Compare the folders D:\Winnt\Users with the list of user account names in User Manager for Domains on the BDC.

   Are there any differences? ____________________

   ____

➤ To test logon hours restrictions

Note Complete this procedure from both computers.

---

1. Attempt to log on as a sales representative.
2. When prompted, change the password to **student**

   Remember, passwords are case-sensitive.

   Were you able to log on successfully? Why or why not?

   ____

   ____

1. Attempt to log on as a customer service (night shift) employee.
2. When prompted, change the password to **student**

   Were you able to log on successfully? Why or why not?

   ____

   ____

➤ To test workstation restrictions

Note Complete this procedure using the temporary employee account that was created by your partner.

1. Log on to your computer as the temporary employee created by your partner.
2. When prompted, change the password to **student**

   Were you able to log on? Why or why not?

   ____

   ____

Lab 2: Configuring User Profiles

Objectives

After completing this lab, you will be able to:

- Define and test a local user profile.
- Define and test a roaming user profile.

Estimated time to complete this lab: 30 minutes

Exercise 1
Defining a Local User Profile

In this exercise, you will work with your partner to create a user account that will be used for a profile template, and then define and test a local user profile.

➤ **To create a user account for a profile template**

Note Complete this procedure from the PDC only.

---

1. Use User Manager for Domains to create a user account named Profile User.
2. Log on as Profile User.
3. Log off Windows NT.

➤ **To use Control Panel to determine existing profiles**

Note Complete the following procedure from both computers.

---

1. Log on as Administrator.
2. Click **Start**, point to **Settings**, click **Control Panel,** and then double-click **System**.

   The **System Properties** dialog box appears.
3. Click **User Profiles**.

   Which users' profiles are stored on your computer?

   ____
4. Click **OK** to close the **Systems Properties** dialog box, and then close Control Panel.

➤ To define and test a local profile

Note Complete the following procedure from both computers.

1. When the previous procedure is complete, log on as the user account that you created for the sales manager.
2. When prompted, change your password to **student**.
3. Right-click anywhere on the desktop, and then on the shortcut menu, click **Properties**.

   The **Display Properties** dialog box appears.
4. Click **Appearance**.

   Notice the current color scheme.
5. In the **Color Schemes** box, select a different color scheme, and then click **OK**.

   The change will take effect immediately.
6. Log off and log on as the same user.

   Were screen colors saved? Why or why not?

   YES
   ____

➤ To compare two local profiles

Note Complete this procedure from the PDC.

1. When the previous procedure is complete, log on as the user account you created for the sales manager.

   Notice that the screen colors are different than when you logged on as the sales manager from the BDC.
2. Right-click anywhere on the desktop, and on the shortcut menu, click **Properties**.

   The **Display Properties** dialog box appears.
3. Click **Appearance**.

   Notice the current color scheme.

   Why is the color scheme different for the sales manager when you view it from the PDC?

   ____
4. Exit all applications and log off Windows NT.

Exercise 2
Defining a Roaming User Profile

In this exercise, you will work with your partner to define a roaming profile by assigning a centralized path to it, and then you will test it by using the profile from multiple computers. Before you test it, you will manually synchronize the PDC's and BDC's directory databases so that both computers will recognize the new profile path immediately.

➤ To assign a roaming profile path

Note Complete this procedure from the BDC.

---

1. Log on as Administrator and start User Manager for Domains.
2. Double-click the account you created for the sales manager.
3. In the **User Properties** dialog box, click **Profile.**
4. In the **User Profile Path** box, type **\\\\student*x*\profiles***sales_manager*
   (where **student***x* is the name of the PDC for your domain and *sales_manager* is the user name you assigned to the sales manager).
5. Click **OK.**
6. Click **OK** again to apply your changes.

➤ To synchronize accounts on the BDC and PDC

Note Complete this procedure from the BDC.

---

1. In Administrative Tools, click Server Manager.

   The Server Manager window appears.
2. Under **Computer**, verify that the PDC in your domain is selected.
3. On the **Computer** menu, click **Synchronize Entire Domain.**

   You receive the following message:

   ```
   Resyncing the DOMAINx domain may take a few minutes. Do you want to
   make the change?
   ```

4. Click **Yes**.

   You receive the following message:

   ```
   The Primary Domain Controller has asked all backup domain controllers
   to start resynchronizing their user accounts databases. Check the
   Event Log on the backup domain controllers and on the Primary Domain
   Controller to determine whether synchronization was successful.
   ```

5. Click **OK**.
6. Exit Server Manager.

➤ To copy a profile template to the shared profile path

In this procedure, you will use the Profile User account (which uses a default profile) to reset the profile for the sales manager.

Note Complete this procedure from the PDC.

---

1. Log on as Administrator and in Control Panel, double-click **System**.
2. Click the **User Profiles** tab.
3. Under **Profiles stored on this computer**, select the user account **Profile User**.
4. Click **Copy To**.
5. In the **Copy profile to** box, type **\\student*x*\profiles***sales_manager* (where **student***x* is the name of the PDC in your domain and *sales_manager* is the user name you assigned to the sales manager).
6. Under **Permitted** to Use, click Change.

   The **Choose User** dialog box appears.
7. Under **Names**, click **Everyone**, and then click **Add**.

   The Everyone group appears in the **Add Name** box.
8. Click **OK** to return to the **Copy to** dialog box.
9. Click **OK** to return to the **System Properties** dialog box.
10. Click **OK** to return to Control Panel.
11. Exit all applications and log off Windows NT.

➤ To test the roaming profile

Note Complete this procedure from the PDC.

1. Log on using the account you created for the sales manager.

   Notice that the screen colors are different than when you logged on as the same user on the BDC. The sales manager's profile has been overwritten with the Profile User's settings.

2. Right-click anywhere on the desktop, and then on the shortcut menu, click **Properties**.

   The **Display Properties** dialog box appears.

3. Click **Appearance**.

   Notice the current color scheme.

4. In the **Color Schemes** box, select a different color scheme than was used on the BDC.

5. Click **Background**, change your wallpaper, and then click **OK**.

   The changes take effect immediately.

6. Exit all applications and log off Windows NT.

➤ To verify that the roaming profile is assigned to the sales manager

Note Complete this procedure from the PDC.

1. Log on as Administrator, and start Control Panel.

2. Double-click **System**, and then click **User Profiles**.

   What type of profile is listed for the sales manager?

   ROAMING
   ____

3. Exit all applications and log off Windows NT.

➤ To test the roaming profile from another computer

Note Complete this procedure from the BDC.

1. Log on using the account you created for the sales manager.
2. If a dialog box appears that provides profile options, click **Download**.

   Are the screen colors and desktop the same or different from those set at the PDC? Why or why not?

   YES

   ---

3. Exit all applications and log off Windows NT.

Lab 3: Planning and Creating Local and Global Groups

Objectives

After completing this lab, you will be able to:

- Plan local and global groups.
- Create global groups and add accounts to them.
- Create local groups and add accounts to them.

Before You Begin

In this lab, you will work with a partner to plan and implement local and global groups for a multiple-domain network.

Estimated time to complete this lab: 45 minutes

Exercise 1
Planning Groups in a Multiple-Domain Network

In this exercise, you will use the following diagram to plan how to implement local and global groups so that users from either domain have access to resources in multiple domains. Record your decisions on the *User and Group Accounts Planning Worksheet.*

You need to determine:

- The global groups for each domain.
- The local groups for each resource, and the computer and domain where they should be created.
- Which global groups to add to each local group to give members access to a resource.

Use the following criteria to make your decisions:

- All employees need access to *Applications* in their own domain.
- All employees need access to the *printer* in the Istanbul domain.
- Executives and managers from both domains need access to the *Human Resources (HR)* information in the Quebec domain.
- Executives, managers, and customer service and sales representatives from both domains need access to the *Customer Files* in the Quebec domain.
- Accountants from both domains need access to *Accounts Receivable (AR)* information in the Quebec domain.

Managers from both domains need access to *Employee Files* in the Istanbul domain.

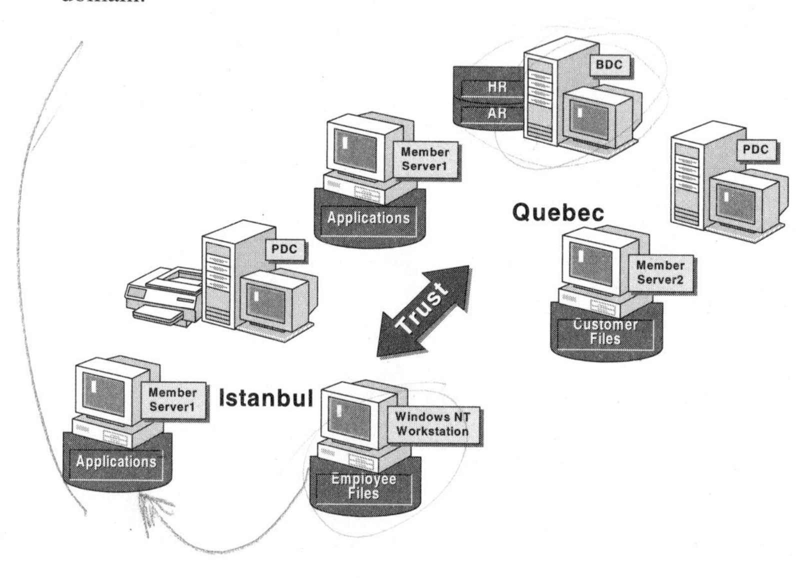

Exercise 2
Creating Global Groups and Adding Members

In this exercise, you will create the global groups you planned for the Quebec domain only. The user accounts that you will add to the global groups are from your *User and Group Accounts Planning Worksheet*.

Important The groups that you planned must be unique to your domain's directory database. Because you and your partner are working in the same domain, you should divide the groups between you. One person can create half of the groups from the BDC and the other person can create the other half from the PDC. Otherwise, only one of you can do the exercise.

➤ **To create a global group**

1. Log on to your domain (DOMAIN*x*, where *x* is the number assigned to your domain) as Administrator.
2. In **Administrative Tools**, start **User Manager for Domains**.
3. On the **User** menu, click **New Global Group**.

   The **New Global Group** dialog box appears.
4. In the **Group Name** box, type a name for your global group (from your *User and Group Accounts Planning Worksheet*).
5. In the **Description** box, type a description for the global group, such as the type of users the group contains.

➤ **To add members to a global group**

1. From the **New Global Group** dialog box, in the **Not Members** box, select one or more users (from your *User and Group Accounts Planning Worksheet*) by pressing the CTRL key, clicking each user, and then clicking **Add**.

   Notice that each new member appears in the **Members** box.
2. Add the remaining user accounts (if any) to the same group, and then click **OK**.

   Notice that the global group appears under **Groups** with a globe as part of the icon.

➤ **To complete the exercise**

- Create the remaining global groups and add members from your *User and Group Accounts Planning Worksheet*.

Exercise 3
Creating Local Groups and Adding Members

In this exercise, you will create the local groups that you planned for the Quebec domain only. You will add to the local groups the global groups that you planned for the Quebec domain only.

Important The groups that you planned must be unique to your domain's directory database, so you and your partner should divide the groups between you. Otherwise, only one of you can do the exercise.

➤ **To create a local group**

1. In the User Manager window, on the **User** menu, click **New Local Group**.

   The **New Local Group** dialog box appears.
2. In the **Group Name** box, type the name for a local group (from your *User and Group Accounts Planning Worksheet*).
3. In the **Description** box, type a description of the local group.

   For example, the description could be the name of the resource to be accessed.

➤ **To add members to a local group**

1. In the **New Local Group** dialog box, click **Add**.

   The **Add Users and Groups** dialog box appears.
2. Under **Names**, click one or more global groups (planned for the Quebec domain only), and then click **Add**.

   Notice that the selected names appear in the **Add Names** box.
3. Click **OK**.

   Notice that the new local group appears under **Groups** with a computer as part of the icon.

➤ **To complete the exercise**

- Create the remaining local groups and add members from your *User and Group Accounts Planning Worksheet.*

Exercise 4
Adding Accounts from a Different Domain

In this exercise, you will add global groups from the CLASSROOMx domain to a local group in your domain (DOMAIN*x*, where *x* is the number assigned to your domain). The CLASSROOM*x* domain (where *x* is the number assigned to the CLASSROOM domain) will act as the Istanbul domain. Your domain will act as the Quebec domain.

Important Because you and your partner are working in the same domain, you should divide the groups between you. Otherwise, only one of you can do the exercise.

➤ **To add a global group from a different domain to a local group**

1. In the User Manager window, double-click the local group you created for the Accounts Receivable (AR) information.

   The **Local Group Properties** dialog box appears.

2. Click **Add**.

   The **Add Users and Groups** dialog box appears.

3. In the **List Names From** box, click **classroom*x***.

   The user and group accounts for the CLASSROOM*x* domain appear in the **Names** list.

4. Double-click the global group **Accountants**, and then click **OK**.

   The Accountants global group appears as a member of your local group.

5. Click **OK** to close the **Local Group Properties** dialog box.

➤ **To complete the exercise**

- Add the following global groups from the CLASSROOM*x* domain to the local groups that you created in your domain.

Add these global groups	To the local group you created for access to
Executives and Managers	Human Resources (HR) information
Executives, Managers, Customer Service, and Sales	Customer files

Exercise 5
Testing Local and Global Group Relationships

In this exercise, you will test four different group combinations to determine whether one group can be added as a member to another group.

- Using User Manager for Domains, try to add each group type listed in the first column to the group type listed in the second column. Write down the results for each combination.

Add this type of group	To this type of group	Result
Global	Global	NO
Global	Local	YES
Local	Local	NO
Local	Global	YES

Lab 4: Implementing Built-in Groups

Objectives

After completing this lab, you will be able to:

- View built-in groups on domain controllers to determine the default members.
- Determine the inherent rights of built-in groups.
- Use the built-in Administrators and Domain Admins groups to administer user accounts in the domain.
- Use the built-in Administrators and Domain Admins groups to provide centralized administration of user accounts in a remote domain.

Estimated time to complete this lab: 30 minutes

Exercise 1
Determining Built-in Group Membership on a Domain Controller

In this exercise, you will view each built-in local and global group on a Microsoft Windows NT Server domain controller to determine the default members.

➤ **To determine membership of the global group Domain Admins**

1. Log on as Administrator.
2. Start User Manager for Domains.
3. Under **Groups**, double-click the global group **Domain Admins**.

   By default, what built-in user accounts or groups are members of Domain Admins?

   Administrator
   ___

4. Click **Cancel** to return to the User Manager window.

➤ **To determine membership of the local group Administrators**

- Under Groups, double-click the local group Administrators.

  By default, what built-in user accounts or global groups are members of the Administrators group?

  Administrator, Domain Admins.
  ___

➤ To determine the default membership of other built-in global groups

- Under Groups, double-click each of the global groups in the following table. Complete the table.

This global group	Contains
Domain Users	administrator + everybody else
Domain Guests	Guest (only)

➤ To determine the default membership of the built-in local group Guests

- Under Groups, double-click Guests.

  What user accounts or groups are members of the Guests group?

  Domain Guests

➤ To determine the default membership of the built-in local group Users

- Under Groups, double-click Users.

  What user accounts or groups are members of the Users group?

  Domain Users

Exercise 2
Determining the Rights of Built-in Groups

In this exercise, you will determine the inherent rights of the built-in local groups.

➤ To determine which groups have access to the computer

- In the User Manager window, on the Policies menu, click User Rights.

  The **User Rights Policy** dialog box appears. The listed right is **Access this computer from network**.

  Which built-in groups have been granted this right?

  Administrator, Everyone

➤ To determine which groups can log on locally

- In the Right box, click Log on locally.

  Which built-in groups have been granted this right?

  Account operators, Administrator, Backup Operators, Everyone, Print operators, server op—

Note The group Everyone does not have the **Log on locally** right by default. This right was assigned to the group during classroom setup.

➤ To determine which groups can change the system time

- In the Right box, click Change the system time.

  Which built-in groups have been granted this right?

➤ To determine which groups can shut down the system

- In the Right box, click Shut down the system.

  Which built-in groups have been granted this right?

➤ **To determine which groups can back up files and directories**

- In the Right box, click Back up files and directories.

  Which built-in groups have been granted this right?

  ____

➤ **To determine which groups can restore files and directories**

- In the Right box, click Restore files and directories.

  Which built-in groups have been granted this right?

  ____

➤ **To determine the inherent rights that are *only* assigned to the Administrators group**

- Select each right to determine which ones are automatically assigned to *only* the Administrators group, and then click the appropriate check boxes.

  Access this computer from network

  Back up files and directories

  Change the system time

  Force shutdown from a remote system

  Load and unload device drivers

  Log on locally

  Manage auditing and security log

  Restore files and directories

  Shut down the system

  Take ownership of files or other objects

Exercise 3
Implementing Built-in Groups for Local Administration

In this exercise, you will work with your partner to add a user account to the local group Administrators and to the global group Domain Admins, and then test the user account group membership. Before you can test the user account from both student computers, you will need to manually synchronize the directory databases.

Note Complete this exercise from the PDC only.

➤ **To create and test a user account**

1. Create a user account.
2. Log on as the new user.
3. Try to create another user account.

   Were you successful? Why or why not?

   No ✓
   ___

➤ **To add a user to the local Administrators group**

1. Log on as Administrator.
2. Add the user you created in the previous procedure to the built-in Administrators group.

➤ **To manually synchronize the directory databases on the BDC and PDC**

- From a command prompt, type net accounts /sync and then press ENTER.

➤ **To test the user account as a member of the Administrators group**

1. Log on as the new user.
2. Try to create another user account.

   Were you successful? Why or why not?

   YES
   ___

➤ **To add a user to the global group Domain Admins**

1. Log on using the default Administrator account.
2. Remove the new user from the Administrators group.
3. Add the new user to the global group Domain Admins.

➤ **To test the user account as a member of the Domain Admins group**

1. Log on as the new user.
2. Try to create another user account.

   Were you successful? Why or why not?

   ____

Exercise 4
Implementing Built-in Groups for Centralized Administration

In this exercise, you will add the Domain Admins group from the CLASSROOM*x* domain (where *x* is the number assigned to the CLASSROOM domain) to the Administrators group in DOMAIN*x* (where *x* is the number assigned to your domain) so that both domains can be administered centrally.

➤ **To test administration of another domain**

Note Complete this procedure from the BDC.

---

1. Log on to the CLASSROOM*x* domain as Administrator.
2. Start User Manager for Domains.
3. On the **User** menu, click **Select Domain**.

   The **Select Domain** dialog box appears.
4. In the **Domain** box, click **DOMAIN***x*.
5. Try to create a user account.

   Were you successful? Why or why not?

   ~~YES~~ NO
   ____

➤ **To add the CLASSROOM*x*\Domain Admins group to the local Administrators group**

Note Complete this procedure from the BDC.

- When the previous procedure is complete, add the Domain Admins group in the CLASSROOM*x* domain (CLASSROOM*x*\Domain Admins) to the local Administrators group.

➤ To test administration of another domain

Note Complete this procedure from the PDC.

---

1. When the previous procedure is complete, log on to the CLASSROOM*x* domain as Administrator.
2. Start User Manager for Domains.
3. On the **User** menu, click **Select Domain**.

   The **Select Domain** dialog box appears.
4. In the **Domain** box, type **domain***x* and then click **OK**.
5. Try again to create a user account.

   Were you successful? Why or why not?

   ____

   ____

   What could you do to enable all administrators to perform administration tasks throughout a domain or in a multiple domain environment?

   ____

   ____

Lab 5: Managing Accounts

Objectives

After completing this lab, you will be able to:

- Assign Account Operator privileges to users.
- Create user account templates.
- Use a template to create user accounts.
- Plan an account policy.
- Set an account policy.
- Unlock a user account.
- Reset a user account password.

Estimated time to complete this lab: 30 minutes

Exercise 1
Assigning Account Operator Privileges to Users

In this exercise, you will add a user to the Account Operators group, and then determine the inherent rights assigned to that group.

➤ To give Account Operator privileges to a user account

1. Log on as Administrator and start User Manager for Domains.
2. Create a user account by typing a name in the **Username** box and leaving the remaining properties blank.
3. Close the **New User** dialog box.
4. In the **Username** list, double-click the account that you just created.
5. In the **User Properties** dialog box, click **Groups**.

   The **Group Memberships** dialog box appears.
6. In the **Not member of** list, click **Account Operators**, and then click **Add**.

   Notice that **Account Operators** appears in the **Member of** list.
7. Click **OK** to close the **Group Memberships** dialog box.
8. Click **OK** to close the **User Properties** dialog box, but do not exit User Manager for Domains.

➤ To manually synchronize domain accounts

- From a command prompt, type **net accounts /sync** and press ENTER to make the account available throughout the domain immediately.

➤ **To determine the inherent rights that are assigned to Account Operators**

1. In the User Manager window, on the **Policies** menu, click **User Rights**.
2. In the **Right** box, select each right one at a time to determine which of the following rights are automatically assigned to the Account Operators group, and then click the appropriate check boxes.

   Access this computer from network

   Add workstations to domain

   Back up files and directories

   Change the system time

   Force shutdown from a remote system

   Load and unload device drivers

   Log on locally

   Manage auditing and security log

   Restore files and directories

   Shut down the system

   Take ownership of files or other objects

3. Click **Cancel**.

Exercise 2
Creating User Account Templates

In this exercise, you will create two user account templates, one for new managers and the other for new night shift employees.

Note This exercise can be done from both computers as long as the names you assign to your templates are unique.

➤ To define the user account template for new managers

1. Log on as the user that you added to the Account Operators group and start User Manager for Domains.
2. When prompted, change the password to **student**
3. In the User Manager window, on the **User** menu, click **New User**.
4. Provide the following information:
   - **Username**: *name* **Template***x* (where *x* is your unique student number)
   - **Description**: (the description that you want to appear for each user account that is created using the template)

Tip Add any valid non-alphabetic character (such as the underscore [_]) as the first character of all template account names to make them appear at the top of the **Username** list.

➤ To define the password requirements for new managers

1. In the **New User** dialog box, make sure that the **User Must Change Password At Next Logon** check box is selected.
2. Select the **Account Disabled** check box.

➤ To define the template home directory path

1. In the **New User** dialog box, click **Profile**.
2. Under **Home Directory**, click **Connect**, and then click **Z**.
3. In the **To** box, type **\\student*x*\users\%username%** (where **student***x* is the name of the PDC in your domain), and then click **OK**.

➤ To define the group accounts for new managers

- Add the managers template to the following groups:
  - The global group you created for Managers.
  - The global group you created for all Quebec domain users (if you decided to use Domain Users, the template account is a member by default).

➤ To define the template for new night shift employees

1. Create a template for the new night shift employees, using the same properties as the managers template (except for groups).
2. Add the night shift employees template to the following groups:
   - The global group you created for customer service employees.
   - The global group you created for all Quebec domain users (if you decided to use Domain Users, the template account is a member by default).
3. Restrict the logon hours for night shift employees to 6:00 P.M. through 6:00 A.M., Monday through Friday.

Exercise 3
Using a Template to Create a User Account

In this exercise, you will use templates to create new user accounts. Then you will compare the options in the new account to the template to determine which options were copied.

➤ **To create a user account using a template**

1. In the User Manager window, under **Username**, select one of your templates.
2. On the **User** menu, click **Copy**.
3. Type a **Username**, **Full Name**, and **Password** for the user, and then click **Add**.
4. Repeat this procedure using the other template you created.

➤ **To determine which account options were copied**

- In the User Manager window, double-click the user account that you created using the night shift employees template. Compare the following options with the template account. Select the appropriate boxes for the options that were copied.

  Username

  Full Name

  Description

  Password and **Confirm Password**

  User Must Change Password at Next Logon

  User Cannot Change Password

  Password Never Expires

  Account Disabled

  Profile

  Groups

  Hours

Exercise 4
Planning an Account Policy

In this exercise, you will work with your partner to plan an account policy for the Quebec domain. You need to determine:

- Password restrictions
- Account lockout requirements

Use the following criteria to make your decisions:

- Users should be required to change their passwords once a month.
- Users should not be able to reuse a password for at least 6 months.
- Every effort should be made to prevent unauthorized users from breaking into the system.
- Employees with restricted logon hours should be disconnected from the network during off hours.

Record your decisions on the following graphic:

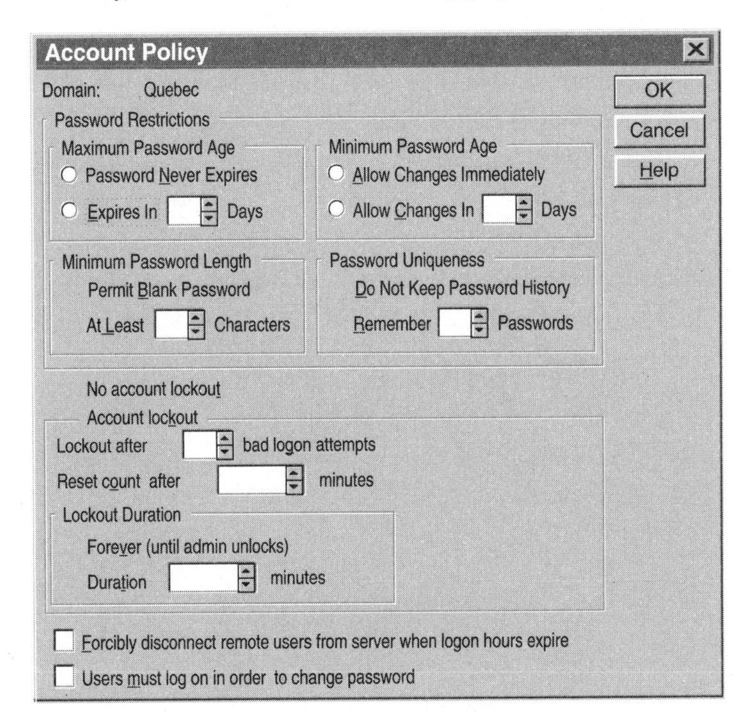

Exercise 5
Setting the Account Policy

In this exercise, you will work with your partner to create an account policy for your domain.

Note Because each domain can have only one account policy, create the account policy from either the PDC or the BDC.

➤ **To set the account policy**

1. Log on as Administrator.
2. In the User Manager window, on the **Policies** menu, click **Account**.

   The **Account Policy** dialog box appears.
3. Set the following account policy for password restrictions and account lockout based on a medium level of security.

Password or account lockout restrictions	Medium security
Maximum Password Age	Expires in 90 days
Minimum Password Age	Allow changes in 30 days
Minimum Password Length	8 characters
Password Uniqueness	Remember 8 passwords
Account Lockout	Yes
Lockout After	3 bad logon attempts
Reset Count After	30 minutes
Lockout Duration	Forever (until administrator unlocks)

4. Click **OK** to set the account policy.

Exercise 6
Testing the Account Policy

In this exercise, you will test the account policy that you established for your domain, including password restrictions and the account lockout option. Because you are checking the account policy you set up, some of the procedures will be based on specific settings in the account policy that you set.

➤ **To test the password restriction portion of the account policy**

1. Create a user account that requires the user to change the password at the next logon.
2. From a command prompt, type **net accounts /sync** to make the account available throughout the domain immediately.
3. Log on as the new user.

   A message box appears, indicating that you are required to change your password at first logon.
4. Click **OK**.
5. In the **New Password** box, type **apple**.
6. In the **Confirm Password** box, type **apple** and then click **OK**.

   Why couldn't you change your password?

   ____
7. Click **OK**.
8. Log on again as the same user. This time, change the password to **watermelon**.

➤ **To test the account lockout portion of the account policy**

1. Log off and try to log on again as the same user, but don't specify a password.

   You should get an error message indicating that the system could not log you on.
2. Click **OK**.
3. Log off and log on two more times with no password.
4. Now log on with the correct password.

   Why couldn't you log on using the correct password?

   ____

   How should the user solve the problem?

   ____
5. Click **OK**.

Exercise 7
Unlocking a Locked Account

In this exercise, you will unlock a locked account.

➤ **To unlock a locked account**

1. Log on as Administrator, and start User Manager for Domains.
2. In the **Username** list, double-click the locked account (from the previous exercise).
3. Clear the **Account Locked Out** check box.
4. Click **OK**.
5. Exit User Manager for Domains.

➤ **To verify that the account is unlocked**

- Log on as the user whose account you unlocked.

Exercise 8
Resetting a User Account Password

In this exercise, you will reset a user account password by deleting the existing password and assigning a new one.

➤ **To reset a user account password**

1. Log on as Administrator.
2. Start User Manager for Domains.
3. Double-click the user account you used in the previous exercise.

   The **User** Properties dialog box appears.
4. In the **Password** box, double-click the entry, and then press the DELETE key.
5. In the **Password** box, type a new password.
6. In the **Confirm Password** box, retype the password, and then click **OK**.
7. Exit User Manager for Domains.

Exercise 9 *(optional)*
Creating Shortcuts to User Manager for Domains

In this exercise, you will create two shortcuts to User Manager for Domains, one to the CLASSROOM*x* domain (where *x* is the number assigned to the Classroom domain) and the other to your domain (DOMAIN*x*, where *x* is the number assigned to your domain).

➤ **To create a shortcut to the CLASSROOM*x* domain**

1. Right-click anywhere on your desktop.
2. On the **User** menu, click **New**, and then click **Shortcut**.
3. In the **Command Line** box, type **Usrmgr classroom***x* and then click **Next**.
4. In the Select a name for the shortcut box, type Classroom*x* and then click Finish.

   The shortcut appears on your desktop.

➤ **To create a shortcut to your domain**

1. Right-click anywhere on your desktop.
2. On the **User** menu, click **New,** and then click **Shortcut**.
3. In the **Command Line** box, type **Usrmgr** and then click **Next**.
4. In the **Select a name for the shortcut** box, type your domain name, and then click **Finish**.

➤ **To test the shortcuts**

- Double-click each shortcut and view the user accounts in each domain.

Lab 6: Managing Domain Controllers

Objectives

After completing this lab, you will be able to:

- Promote a BDC to a PDC when the PDC is online.
- Promote a BDC to a PDC when the PDC is offline.
- Restore a PDC.
- Synchronize domain controllers.
- Troubleshoot problems related to users logging on to the network.

Before You Begin

In this lab, you will work with a partner. Many of the procedures in the exercises will be done from only one of the computers. Work with your domain partner so that you both gain experience.

You will need to know the roles of your domain controllers. The roles of your domain controllers will change during this lab.

Your computers will be identified by their roles—primary domain controller (PDC) or backup domain controller (BDC).

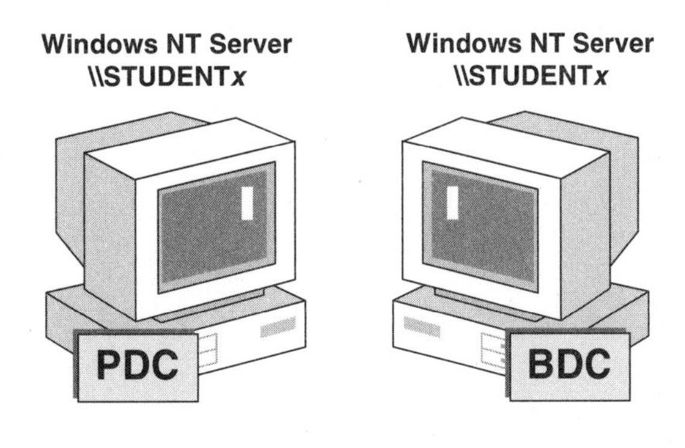

Estimated time to complete this lab: 45 minutes

Exercise 1
Promoting a BDC to a PDC When the PDC Is Online

In this exercise, you will promote a BDC to the role of PDC based on the following scenario.

Scenario

Your PDC needs to be taken offline for some routine maintenance. You will use Server Manager to promote a BDC to a PDC and then demote the original PDC to a BDC. When this is accomplished, you can then take the original PDC offline for maintenance.

➤ **To verify server roles and information**

Note Complete this procedure from both computers.

1. Log on to your domain as Administrator.
2. In **Administrative Tools**, start **Server Manager**.
3. Complete the following table about the servers in your domain.

Computer	Type
Student09	Primary
student10	Backup

What appears differently about each computer type?

Little window shows up on Backup

Does this information match the information that appears in Server Manager on the other computer in your domain? Why or why not?

YES

➤ To promote a BDC to a PDC

Note Complete this procedure from the BDC only.

1. In Server Manager, select the BDC.
2. On the Computer menu, click Promote to Primary Domain Controller.
3. When prompted for confirmation of the change, click **Yes**.

   The Server Manager status box appears. Notice the actions that are occurring during the promotion.

   When this procedure is finished, the original PDC automatically becomes a BDC.

➤ To refresh a Server Manager window

Note Complete this procedure from the new PDC only.

- Press F5 to refresh the Server Manager window.

➤ To verify server information

Note Complete this procedure from both computers.

- Use Server Manager to complete the following table about the servers in your domain.

Computer	Type

Does this information match the information on the other domain controller in your domain? Why or why not?

____

How does this information compare to the information in the first procedure?

____

➤ To return the BDC to PDC status

Note Complete this procedure from the PDC only.

1. In Server Manager, select the BDC (the original PDC).
2. Promote the BDC to a primary domain controller.

   Notice that the PDC was automatically demoted to a BDC.

Important Complete this procedure from the PDC only.

Exercise 2
Promoting a BDC to a PDC When the PDC Is Offline

In this exercise, you will promote a BDC to the role of PDC based on the following scenario.

Scenario

Your primary domain controller is offline. The computer failed, and when you ran diagnostics on it, you discovered that some of the memory was corrupted. It will take a week before you can get the replacement memory chips, so you need to use Server Manager to promote a BDC to a PDC.

➤ **To take the PDC offline**

Note Complete this procedure from the PDC only.

---

1. Press CTRL+ALT+DELETE to open the **Windows NT Security** dialog box.
2. Click Shut down.
3. When prompted to shut down the computer, click **Shutdown**, and then click **OK**.
4. Turn off the computer when the shutdown process is finished.

➤ **To promote a BDC to a PDC**

Note Complete this procedure from the BDC only.

---

1. In **Server Manager**, click the BDC.
2. On the Computer menu, click **Promote to Primary Domain Controller**.

   The following message appears:

   ```
   Promoting STUDENTx to Primary may take a few minutes. Do you want to
   make the change?
   ```

3. Click **Yes**.

   The following message appears:

   ```
   Cannot find the Primary for DOMAINx. Continuing with the promotion
   may result in errors when DOMAINx's old Primary comes back online. Do
   you want to continue with the promotion?
   ```

4. Click **OK**.

Exercise 3
Restoring a PDC

In this exercise, you will return the original PDC to its role of PDC by:

- Restarting the original PDC.
- Demoting the original PDC to a BDC.

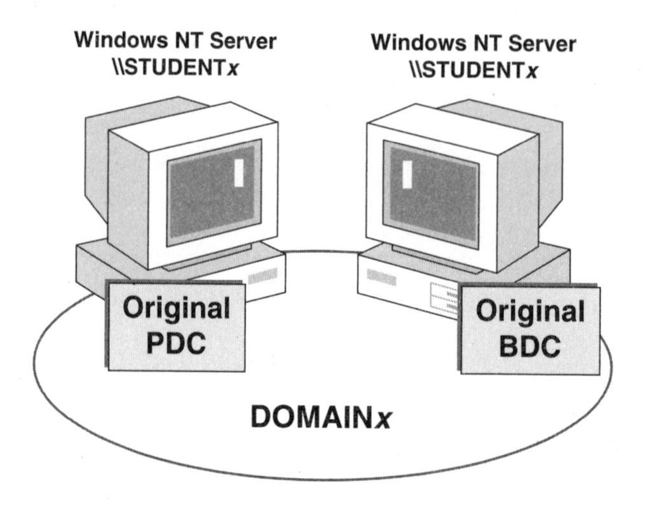

➤ **To restart a PDC**

Note Complete this procedure from the original PDC only.

---

1. Start the original PDC and log on as Administrator.

   A message appears, indicating that at least one service or driver failed. This is because the original PDC was unable to assume the role of PDC. There was already a PDC in the domain, causing the Netlogon service to fail.

2. Click **OK**.

➤ To switch roles by demoting the original PDC to a BDC

1. Start Server Manager.

   Notice that both the original PDC and the current PDC are listed as primary domain controllers, but the icon for the original PDC is unavailable.

2. Select the original PDC.
3. On the **Computer** menu, click **Demote to Backup Domain Controller**.
4. When prompted, click **Yes** to make the change.
5. Select the original PDC (which is the current BDC).
6. On the **Computer** menu, click **Promote to Primary Domain Controller**.
7. When prompted, click **Yes** to make the change.

   Notice that the original BDC is demoted back to BDC.

Exercise 4
Synchronizing Domain Controllers

In this exercise, you will observe what may happen when a domain is not synchronized. You will then synchronize the domain controllers in your domain.

➤ To prepare to test synchronization

Note Complete this procedure from the BDC.

- Log off the BDC.

➤ To create a new user account

Note Complete this procedure from the PDC.

---

1. Using User Manager for Domains, create a new user account.

   Do not require the user to change the password the next time the user logs on.
2. Proceed immediately to the next procedure.

➤ To verify that the domain is out of synchronization

Note Complete this procedure from the BDC.

- Immediately log on as the new user.

  Were you successful? Why or why not?

  No,

➤ To synchronize the domain

Note Complete this procedure from the PDC. You should be logged on as Administrator.

---

1. In Server Manager, select the BDC.
2. On the **Computer** menu, click **Synchronize with Primary Domain Controller**.

   A Server Manager message appears, indicating that the synchronization might take a few minutes, and asking you to confirm the change.

3. When prompted, click **Yes** to make the change.

   The Server Manager information box appears, indicating that synchronization has started.

4. Click **OK**.
5. Wait approximately 30 seconds, and then proceed.

➤ To verify that the domain is synchronized

Note Complete this procedure from the BDC only.

1. Log on as the new user.

   Were you successful? Why or why not?

   ____

2. Log off and log on as Administrator.

➤ To verify synchronization using Event Viewer

Note Complete this procedure from both computers.

1. In Administrative Tools, click Event Viewer.
2. On the **Log** menu, click **System**.

   The System event log appears.

3. Under **Source**, select the most recent NETLOGON event.
4. On the **View** menu, click **Detail**.
5. Read the event details by clicking **Next** until you find confirmation of synchronization.

   How many changes were synchronized?

   1 change ______________________________

6. Exit Event Viewer.

Exercise 5
Troubleshooting User Logon Problems

In this exercise, you will troubleshoot two problems related to users logging on to the network. To produce each problem, you will run a batch file from the PDC. You will solve the problems from both computers.

Scenario 1

You have just added a new user account, and you need to test it before allowing the user to use the account. The user account for the PDC is *PDC1* and the password is *password*. The user account for the BDC is *BDC1* and the password is *password*.

➤ **To produce the problem (from the PDC only)**

1. Log on as Administrator.
2. From a command prompt, type **d:\labfiles\1** and then press ENTER.

➤ **To test the problem**

- Log on using the following user names:
  - On the PDC, log on as PDC1.
  - On the BDC, log on as BDC1.

  What is the symptom of the problem?

  Couldn't Log on

➤ **To solve the problem**

- Use User Manager for Domains to determine the problem and solve it.

  What is the problem?

  What is the solution to the problem?

Scenario 2

Two users need to change their passwords, but they are having problems logging on. The user account for the PDC is *PDC2* and the password is *password*. The user account for the BDC is *BDC2* and the password is *password*. They need to change their passwords to match their user names.

➤ **To produce the problem (from the PDC only)**

1. Log on as Administrator.
2. From a command prompt, type **d:\labfiles\2** and then press ENTER.

➤ **To test the problem (from both computers)**

- Log on using the names specified in the scenario:
  - On the PDC, log on as PDC2.
  - On the BDC, log on as BDC2.

  What is the symptom of the problem?

  ___

  ___

➤ **To solve the problem**

- Use User Manager for Domains to determine the problem and solve it.

  What is the problem?

  ___

  ___

  What is the solution to the problem?

  ___

  ___

Lab 7: Planning Shared Folders

Objectives

After completing this lab, you will be able to:

- Plan shared folders.
- Plan user and group permissions.

Before You Begin

In this lab, you will work with your partner to plan a folder hierarchy and permissions.

Estimated time to complete this lab: 30 minutes

Exercise 1
Planning Shared Folders

In this exercise, you will work with a partner to plan how to share resources on servers in the Istanbul office of World Wide Importers. You will record your decisions on the *Network Resources Planning Worksheet 1.*

The following diagram shows the servers in the office.

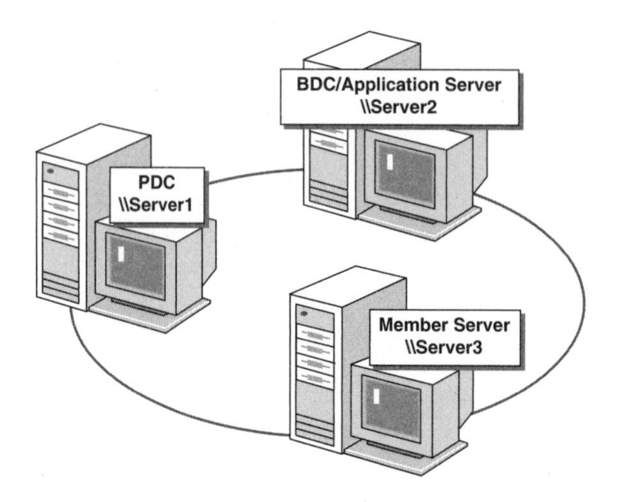

This server	Has this folder structure
\\Server1	\Users\%USERNAME%
\\Server2	\Data\Accntg \Data\HR \Reviews
\\Server3	\Apps\Spreadsh \Apps\WordProc \Apps\Database \ProjMan

You need to make resources on these servers available to network users. To do this, you need to determine:

- What folders to share.
- What groups to create, what built-in groups to use, and the appropriate permissions for each.
- A public folder location for users to share information.

The decisions you make are based on the following criteria:

- All employees need access to the spreadsheet, database, and word processing software.
- Only managers should be able to access the project management software.
- All employees need a network location to share information.
- The Accounting and Human Resources departments require their own network location to store their working files. Executives require access to these locations.
- Managers and executives require a network location to store employee performance reviews.
- Each user needs a private network location to store files. This location must be accessible only by that user.
- Share names must be accessible from Microsoft Windows NT, Microsoft Windows 95, and non-Windows NT platforms.

Lab 8: Sharing Folders

Objectives

After completing this lab, you will be able to:

- Share a folder.
- Assign shared folder permissions to users and groups.
- Connect to a shared folder.
- Stop sharing a folder.

Estimated time to complete this lab: 30 minutes

Exercise 1
Sharing Folders

In this exercise, you will share folders and assign permissions.

➤ **To share a folder**

1. Log on as Administrator, and start Windows NT Explorer.
2. Expand D:\LabFiles, right-click the Apps folder, and then click **Properties**.

   The **Apps Properties** dialog box appears.
3. Click the **Sharing** tab.

Tip When you right-click the Apps folder, notice that the **Sharing** command appears on the shortcut menu. If you click **Sharing** on this menu, you will switch directly to the **Sharing** tab of the **Apps Properties** dialog box.

---

4. Click **Shared As**.

   Notice that the **Share Name** defaults to the name of the folder.
5. In the **Comment** box, type **Shared Productivity Applications** and then click **OK**.

   Looking at Windows NT Explorer, what appears in the Apps folder indicating that it is shared?

   A hand underneath the folder
   ___

Exercise 2
Assigning Shared Folder Permissions

In this exercise, you will determine the current permissions for a shared folder, and assign shared folder permissions to groups in the default domain and to a global group in a different domain.

➤ To determine the current permissions for the Apps shared folder

1. In Windows NT Explorer, right-click the Apps folder, and then click **Sharing**.

   The **Apps Properties** dialog box appears.

2. Click **Permissions**.

   The **Access Through Share Permissions** dialog box appears.

   What are the default permissions for the Apps shared folder?

   Everyone
   ___

➤ To remove permissions for a group

- In the **Access Through Share Permissions** dialog box, under **Names**, make sure **Everyone** is selected, and then click **Remove**.

➤ To assign Full Control permission to the Administrators group

1. In the Access Through Share Permissions dialog box, click Add.

   The **Add Users and Groups** dialog box appears.

   What domain name appears in the **List Names From** box?

   Domain09
   ___

2. Under **Names**, click **Administrators**, and then click **Add**.

   What appears in the **Add Names** box to indicate the location of the directory database where the selected name resides?

   DOMAIN09\ Administrator
   ___

3. In the **Type Of Access** box, select **Full Control**, and then click **OK**.

   The **Access Through Share Permissions** dialog box reappears. Notice that the Administrators group has Full Control permission.

➤ To assign permissions in a multiple-domain network

1. In the Access Through Share Permissions dialog box, click Add.

   The **Add Users and Groups** dialog box appears.

2. Click the **List Names From** arrow to display the list of other domains from which you can select user names for assigning permissions.

   What domains are available?

   DOMAIN 09, CLASSROOM

3. Click **CLASSROOM***x* (where *x* is the number assigned to the classroom domain).

   Notice the list of Global groups for the CLASSROOM*x* domain.

4. Click **Students**, and then click **Add**.

   Notice that CLASSROOM*x*\Students appears under **Add Names**.

5. In the **Type Of Access** box, make sure the **Read** permission is selected, and then click **OK**.

   The **Access Through Share Permissions** dialog box appears. Notice that the Students group from the CLASSROOM*x* domain appears with Read permissions.

➤ To assign permissions to a user account in a different domain

1. In the Access Through Share Permissions dialog box, click Add.

   The **Add Users and Groups** dialog box appears.

2. Click the **List Names From** arrow, and then click **CLASSROOM***x*.

   The list of global groups for CLASSROOM*x* appears.

3. Click **Show Users**, and then scroll to the bottom of the list.

   Notice that the user accounts for the CLASSROOM*x* domain appear.

4. Click **Student***x* (where *x* is your student number), and then click **Add**.

5. In the **Type Of Access** box, click **Change**, and then click **OK** twice.

   The **Apps Properties** dialog box appears.

6. Click **OK** to apply your changes.

7. Exit Windows NT Explorer.

Exercise 3
Connecting to a Shared Folder

In this exercise, you will use two methods to connect to a shared folder. You will then use **Connect as** to specify a different user account to connect to a shared folder.

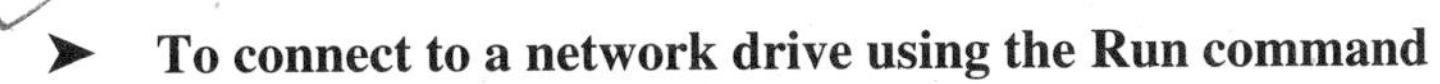

➤ To connect to a network drive using the Run command

1. Click **Start**, and then click **Run**.
2. In the **Open** box, type **\\instructor***x* (where *x* is the number assigned to the instructor's computer) and then click **OK**.

   The Instructor*x* window appears.

   Notice that only the folders that are shared appear to network users.
3. Close the Instructor*x* window.

➤ To connect a network drive to a shared folder using Map Network Drive

1. On the desktop, right-click **Network Neighborhood**, and then click **Map Network Drive**.
2. In the **Drive** box, click **P**.
3. In the Path box, type **\\instructor***x***\public**.
4. Clear the **Reconnect at Logon** check box, and then click **OK**.
5. Close the Public on 'Instructor*x*' (P:) window.
6. Start Windows NT Explorer and view the drives under My Computer.

   Notice that drive P has been added as Public on 'Instructor*x*' (P:).

➤ To disconnect a network drive using Windows NT Explorer

1. In Windows NT Explorer, right-click drive **P**.
2. Click **Disconnect**.

   Drive P is removed from the left pane of Windows NT Explorer.
3. Exit Windows NT Explorer and log off.

➤ To attempt to connect to a shared folder on Instructor*x*

1. Log on as Student*x* in the CLASSROOM*x* domain, with no password.
2. Make sure that Windows NT Explorer is not running.
3. Right-click **Network Neighborhood**, and then click **Map Network Drive**.

   The **Map Network Drive** dialog box appears.
4. In the **Drive** box, click **S**.
5. In the Path box, type **\\\\instructor*x*\\security**
6. Click to clear the **Reconnect at Logon** check box, and then click **OK**.

   You receive a message stating that access is denied.

   Why weren't you able to access the Security shared folder?

   Because! security is not shared
7. In the **Security on 'Instructor*x*' (S:)** dialog box, click **Cancel**.
8. Right-click **Network Neighborhood**, and then click **Disconnect Network Drive**.

   The **Disconnect Network Drive** dialog box appears.
9. Under **Network Drive**, click **S: \\\\Instructor*x*\\Security,** and then click **OK** to disconnect the drive.

➤ To connect to a shared folder using another user account

1. Right-click Network Neighborhood, and then click Map Network Drive.

   The **Map Network Drive** dialog box appears.
2. In the **Drive** box, click **S**.
3. In the **Path** box, type **\\\\instructor*x*\\security**
4. In the **Connect as** box, type **Classroom*x*\\administrator**
5. Click to clear the **Reconnect at Logon** check box, and then click **OK**.
6. If you are prompted to enter a network password, type **password**

   Can you access the Security share? Why or why not?

   NO!
7. Exit Windows NT Explorer.

Exercise 4
Testing the Shared Folder Permissions

In this exercise, you will connect to shared folders and observe the effects of assigned permissions using accounts from the CLASSROOM*x* domain. Student*x* is a member of the Students group. For this exercise, the Students group has Read permission to the \Instructor*x*\Apps folder.

Note Complete this exercise while logged on as Student*x* in the CLASSROOM*x* domain.

➤ **To test shared folder permissions by logging on to another domain**

1. Right-click Network Neighborhood, and then click Map Network Drive.
2. In the **Drive** box, click **T**.
3. In the **Path** box, type *partner's_server***Apps**
4. Click to clear the **Reconnect at Logon** check box, and then click **OK**.

   Were you successful? Why or why not?

   YES

   A window for the mapped drive appears.

➤ **To test shared folder permissions by running an application**

1. In the Apps window, expand the \Games folder and run Kolumz.exe.

   Were you successful? Why or why not?

   YES

2. Exit Kolumz.exe.

➤ **To test shared folder permissions**

1. In Windows NT Explorer, delete Kolumz.exe.

   Were you successful? Why or why not?

   YES

2. Exit Windows NT Explorer and log off.

Exercise 5
Stopping a Shared Folder

In this exercise, you will stop sharing a shared folder.

Note Wait until the previous exercise has been completed at both the PDC and BDC before continuing.

➤ **To stop sharing a folder**

1. Log on to your domain as Administrator, and then start Windows NT Explorer.
2. Expand drive D, right-click the Apps folder, and then click **Sharing**.

   The **Sharing** tab of the **Apps Properties** dialog box appears.
3. Click **Not Shared,** and then click **OK**.

   Notice that the hand no longer appears on the Apps folder.

Exercise 6 *(optional)* Creating Hidden Shared Folders

In this exercise, you will create a hidden share on your server and then test it to verify that it is actually hidden.

➤ To create a folder and a hidden share name

1. Start Windows NT Explorer and select drive C.
2. On the **File** menu, click **New**, and then click **Folder** to create a new folder.
3. Type **Secret** for the folder name, and then press ENTER.

   A folder named Secret appears under **Contents of (C:)**.
4. Right-click the Secret folder, and then click **Sharing**.

   The **Secret Properties** dialog box appears.
5. Click **Shared As**.

   Notice that the share name defaults to the name Secret.
6. In the **Share Name** box, type **Secret$**

   The $ makes the share name hidden to network users.
7. In the **Comment** box, type **System Utilities** and then click **OK**.

   Notice that Windows NT Explorer shows a hand holding the Secret folder, indicating that the folder is shared.

➤ To test the visibility of the hidden share name

1. Click **Start,** and then click **Run**.
2. In the **Open** box, type **\\student***x* and then click **OK**.
3. Does the **Secret$** share appear?

   NO
   ___
4. Exit all applications.

➤ To connect to a hidden shared folder

1. Click **Start**, and then click **Run**.
2. In the **Open** box, type **\\student***x***\secret$** (where **student***x* is your partner's computer) and then click **OK**.

   Were you able to access the **Secret$** share? Why or why not?

   ___
3. Exit Windows NT Explorer and log off Windows NT.

Lab 9: Planning and Assigning NTFS Permissions Objectives

After completing this lab, you will be able to:

- Plan NTFS file and folder permissions for a folder hierarchy.
- Assign NTFS and shared folder permissions to a folder hierarchy.

Estimated time to complete this lab: 45 minutes

Exercise 1
Planning NTFS Folder and File Permissions

In this exercise, you will work with a partner to plan how to assign NTFS permissions and share resources on a computer running Windows NT Server, based on the following folder hierarchies.

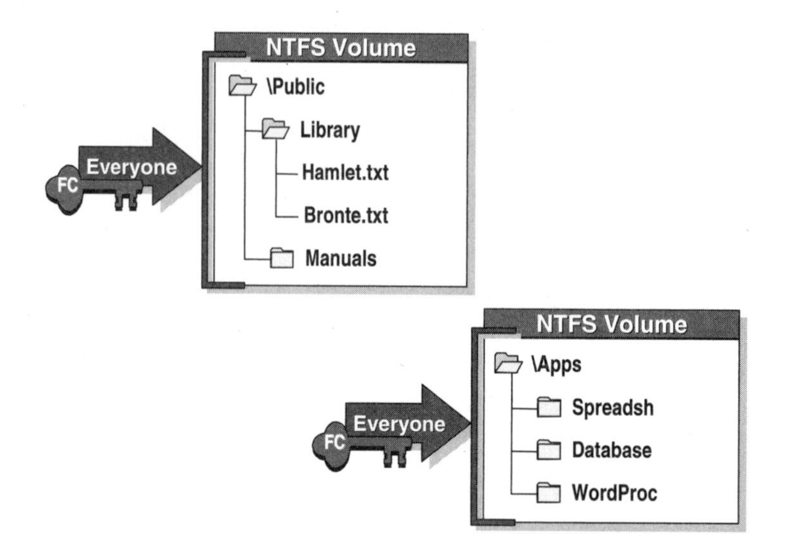

Record your decisions for the path, folder name, users and groups, and permissions on the *Network Resources Planning Worksheet 2.*

You need to make the resources on the computer available to network users, and secure these resources according to the needs of the company. (The volume has been formatted with NTFS.) To do this you need to determine:

- What groups to create and what built-in groups to use.
- What permissions users will require to gain access to the appropriate folders and files.

The decisions you make are based on the following criteria:

- Share names must be accessible from Windows NT, Windows 95, and non-Windows NT platforms.
- Administrators require Full Control access to all folders and files.
- All users will run programs in the WordProc folder, but they should not be able to modify the files in the WordProc folder.
- Only members of the Accounting, Managers, and Executives groups should be able to access the Spreadsh and Database application folders, but they should not be able to modify the files in those folders.
- All users should be able to create and modify their files in the \Public folder, but they should be not be able to modify other users' files.
- All users should be prevented from modifying files in the \Public\Library folder.
- Only UserA should be able to modify files in the \Public\Manuals folder.

Exercise 2
Assigning NTFS Permissions to a Public Folder

In this exercise, you will assign NTFS permissions to the Public folder based on your *Network Resources Planning Worksheet 2*. The Public folder is located in D:\LabFiles.

➤ **To assign permissions to Users for the Public folder**

1. Log on as Administrator and start Windows NT Explorer.
2. Right-click the D:\LabFiles\Public folder, and then on the shortcut menu, click **Properties**.
3. Click the **Security** tab, and then click **Permissions**.

   The **Directory Permissions** dialog box appears.

   What are the existing folder permissions?

   Everyone
   ___
4. In the **Directory Permissions** dialog box, click **Add**.

   The **Add Users and Groups** dialog box appears.
5. Under **Names**, click **Users**, and then click **Add**.

   DOMAIN*x*\Users appears under **Add Names**.
6. In the **Type Of Access** box, click **Add & Read**, and then click **OK**.

   The **Directory Permissions** dialog box appears.
7. Under **Name**, click **Everyone**, and then click **Remove**.

➤ **To assign permissions to Creator Owner for the Public folder**

1. In the **Directory Permissions** dialog box, click **Add**.

   The **Add Users and Groups** dialog box appears.
2. Under **Names**, click **Creator Owner**, and then click **Add**.
3. In the **Type Of Access** box, click **Full Control**, and then click **OK**.

   The **Directory Permissions** dialog box appears.

➤ To assign permissions to Administrators for the Public folder

1. In the **Directory Permissions** dialog box, click **Add**.

   The **Add Users and Groups** dialog box appears.

2. Under **Names**, click **Administrators**, and then click **Add**.
3. In the **Type Of Access** box, click **Full Control**, and then click **OK**.

   In the **Directory Permissions** dialog box, notice that the Administrators group and Creator Owner have Full Control permission, and that the Users group has the Add & Read permission.

4. Select the **Replace Permissions on Subdirectories** check box. Verify that the **Replace Permissions on Existing Files** check box is selected, and then click **OK**.

   The following message appears:

   ```
   Do you want to replace the security information on all existing
   subdirectories within D:\LabFiles\Public?
   ```

5. Click **Yes** to return to the **Public Properties** dialog box, and then click **OK** to apply your changes.
6. Create a file in D:\LabFiles\Public.

➤ To test the folder permissions assigned for Public

1. Log on as the day shift customer service representative you created in Lab 1: Planning and Creating User Accounts, and start Windows NT Explorer.
2. Expand the D:\LabFiles\Public folders.
3. Attempt to create a file in the Public folder.

   Were you successful? Why or why not?

   YES! grant permission to all users (add x read)

4. Attempt to perform the following tasks for the file that you just created and record those that you are able to complete.

   Open the file YES

   Modify the file YES

   Delete the file YES

   FULL CONTROL

5. Attempt to perform the following tasks for the file created by the administrator and record those tasks that you are able to complete.

   Open the file____________

   Modify the file____________

   Delete the file____________

6. Exit all applications and log off.

➤ To share the Public folder

1. Log on as Administrator, start Windows NT Explorer, and share the Public folder.
2. Assign the Users group Full Control permission to the Public shared folder.
3. Remove the Everyone group from the shared Public folder.
4. Exit all applications and log off.

➤ To test the remote folder permissions assigned for Public

Note Wait until the previous procedure has been completed on both the PDC and BDC before starting this procedure.

---

1. Log on as the day shift customer service representative you created in Lab 1: Planning and Creating User Accounts.
2. Click **Start,** and then click **Run**.
3. In the **Open** box, type **\\Student*x*\Public** (where **student*x*** is your partner's computer) and then click **OK**.

   The Public on Student*x* window appears.
4. Attempt to create a file in the Public folder.

   Were you successful? Why or why not?

   YES!
   ____
5. Attempt to perform the following tasks for the file that your *partner* created while logged on as administrator and record those that you are able to complete.

   Open the file___✓___

   Modify the file___✓___

   Delete the file___✓___
6. Close Windows NT Explorer and log off.

Exercise 3
Assigning NTFS Permissions and Sharing Folders

In this exercise, you will assign NTFS permissions to the Apps, Library, and Manuals folders based on your *Network Resources Planning Worksheet 2*. You will then share application folders. The Apps, Library, and Manuals folders are located in D:\LabFiles.

➤ To assign NTFS permissions

1. Log on as Administrator and create a user named UserA.
2. Start Windows NT Explorer and expand drive D.
3. Right-click the folder or file, and then click **Properties**.

   The *Folder/File_name* **Properties** dialog box appears.
4. In the *Folder/File_name* **Properties** dialog box, click the **Security** tab, and then click **Permissions**.
5. Configure the following options.

For this option	Do this
Replace permissions on subdirectories	Select this check box.
Replace permissions on existing files	Select this check box.

6. To add permissions for users or local groups to the folder or file, click **Add**.
7. Configure the **Add Users and Groups** box to assign permissions to the appropriate local groups or users based on the *Network Resources Planning Worksheet 2.*

➤ To share folders and assign shared folder permissions

- Share the appropriate application folders and assign network users permissions based on the *Network Resources Planning Worksheet 2.*

Exercise 4
Testing Permissions

In this exercise, you will log on as various users and test permissions.

➤ **To test permissions for the Manuals folder when a user logs on locally**

1. Log on as the day shift customer service representative you created in Lab 1: Planning and Creating User Accounts, and start Windows NT Explorer.
2. In Windows NT Explorer, expand the D:\LabFiles\Public\Manuals folder.
3. Attempt to create a file in the Manuals folder.

   Were you successful? Why or why not?

   ____

Note Wait until the previous procedure has been completed on both the PDC and BDC before continuing.

➤ **To test permissions for the Manuals folder when a user connects over the network**

1. Click **Start**, and then click **Run**.
2. In the **Open** box, type **\\Student*x*\Public** (where *x* is your student number) and then click **OK**.

   The Public on Student*x* window appears.
3. In the Public on Student*x* window, expand your partner's Manuals folder.
4. Attempt to create a file in the Manuals folder on your partner's computer.

   Were you successful? Why or why not?

   ____

   ____

➤ **To test permissions for the Manuals folder when logged on as UserA**

1. Log on as UserA and start Windows NT Explorer.
2. Expand the D:\LabFiles\Public\Manuals folder.
3. Attempt to create a file in the Manuals folder.

   Were you successful? Why or why not?

   ____

4. Connect to the Public shared folder on your partner's computer.

   The Public on Student*x* window appears.

5. Attempt to create a file in the Manuals folder on your partner's computer.

   Were you successful? Why or why not?

   ____

   ____

➤ **To test permissions for the Apps folder while logged on locally as Administrator**

1. Log on as Administrator and start Windows NT Explorer.
2. Expand the D:\LabFiles\Apps folder.
3. Attempt to create a file in the WordProc folder.

   Were you successful? Why or why not?

   ____

4. Attempt to create a file in the Spreadsh folder and then in the Database folder.

   Were you successful? Why or why not?

   ____

5. Exit Windows NT Explorer and log off.

➤ **To test permissions for application folders when a user logs on locally**

1. Log on as the day shift customer service representative you created in Lab 1: Planning and Creating User Accounts, and start Windows NT Explorer.
2. Expand the D:\LabFiles\Apps folder.
3. Attempt to create a file in the WordProc folder.

   Were you successful? Why or why not?

   ____

   ____

➤ To test permissions for application folders when a user connects over the network

1. Connect to the Apps shared folder on your partner's computer.

   The Apps on Student*x* window appears.
2. Attempt to create a file in the WordProc folder.

   Were you successful? Why or why not?

   ____

   ____
3. In the WordProc folder, attempt to open the file that you created in the previous procedure.

   Were you successful? Why or why not?

   ____

   ____

➤ To modify permissions for the Apps shared folder

1. Log on as Administrator and start Windows NT Explorer.
2. Right-click the D:\LabFiles\Apps folder, and then, on the shortcut menu, click **Sharing**.
3. Click **Permissions**.

   The **Access Through Share Permissions** dialog box appears.
4. Click **Users**, and then, in the **Type Of Access** box, click **Read**.
5. Click **OK** to return to the **Apps Properties** dialog box.
6. Click **OK** to apply your changes.

➤ To test permissions for the Apps shared folder

Note Wait until the previous procedure has been completed on both the PDC and BDC before continuing.

1. Connect to your partner's Apps shared folder.
2. Attempt to create a file in the WordProc folder.

   Were you successful? Why or why not?

   ____
3. Attempt to create a file in the Spreadsh folder, and then in the Database folder.

   Were you successful? Why or why not?

   ____

Lab 10: Managing Permissions

Objectives

After completing this lab, you will be able to:

- Take ownership of a file.
- Copy and move folders and files.
- Identify and solve permission-related problems.

Estimated time to complete this lab: 45 minutes

Exercise 1
Taking Ownership of a File

In this exercise, you will log on as a user and observe the effects of taking ownership of a file. To do this, you will determine permissions for a file, assign permission to a user to take ownership, and take ownership as that user.

➤ **To determine the permissions for a file**

1. Log on as Administrator and start Windows NT Explorer.
2. In the D:\LabFiles\Public folder, create a text file named Owner.txt
3. Right-click **Owner.txt**, and then click **Properties**.

   The **Owner.txt Properties** dialog box appears.
4. Click **Security**, and then click **Ownership**.

   Who is the current owner of Owner.txt?

   [illegible] ____________________
5. Click **Close**, and then click **Permissions**.

   What are the current permissions for Owner.txt?

   full control ____________________

➤ **To assign permission to a user to take ownership**

1. In the **File Permissions** dialog box, click **Add**.

   The **Add Users and Groups** dialog box appears.
2. Click **Show Users**.
3. Select the user you created for the Sales Manager, and then click **Add**.
4. In the **Type Of Access** box, click **Read**, and then click **OK.**

   The **File Permissions** dialog box appears.
5. In the **Name** box, click the user account you created for the Sales Manager.
6. In the **Type Of Access** box, click **Special Access**.

   The **Special Access** dialog box appears.

   What permissions are already selected? Why?

   read, execute ____________________

   ____
7. Select the **Take Ownership (O)** check box, click **OK** three times to apply your changes, and then exit to Windows NT Explorer.
8. Exit all applications and log off.

➤ To take ownership of a file

1. Log on as the Sales Manager and start Windows NT Explorer.
2. Expand the D:\LabFiles\Public folder.
3. Right-click the file **Owner.txt**, and then click **Properties**.

   The **Owner.txt Properties** dialog box appears.
4. On the **Security** tab, click **Ownership**.
5. In the **Owner** dialog box, click **Take Ownership**.
6. On the **Security** tab, click **Ownership**.

   Who is the owner of Owner.txt?

   Sales Manager (Pam Smith)

   Why could the Sales Manager take ownership of Owner.txt?

   Granted to do so

➤ To test permissions to a file as the owner

1. Assign the Sales Manager the Full Control permission to the file Owner.txt.
2. Remove permissions for all users and groups from the file Owner.txt.

   Were you successful? Why or why not?

   YES! Sales Manager is the owner of the file

Exercise 2
Copying and Moving Folders

In this exercise, you will see the effects of permissions and ownership when copying and moving folders. To do this, you will create a folder while logged on as a user, and while logged on as Administrator.

➤ To create a folder while logged on as a user

Note Complete this procedure while logged on as the sales manager.

1. In D:\, create a folder named Temp1.

   What are the permissions assigned to the folder?

   Full control to everyone

   Who is the owner? Why?

   Sales manager!

2. Log off.

➤ To create a folder while logged on as Administrator

1. Log on as Administrator and start Windows NT Explorer.
2. In D:\, create the following folders:
   - Temp2
   - Temp3

   What are the permissions of the folders that you just created?

   Full control to everyone

   Who is the owner of the D:\Temp2 and D:\Temp3 folders? Why?

   administrator! Created by administrator.

3. Remove the group Everyone and assign the following permissions to the D:\Temp2 and D:\Temp3 folders.

Folder	Assign these permissions
D:\Temp2	Administrators: Full Control Users: Read
D:\Temp3	Backup Operators: Read Users: Full Control

➤ To copy a folder to another folder within an NTFS volume

1. Copy D:\Temp2 to D:\Temp1.
2. Select D:\Temp1\Temp2 and compare the permissions and ownership with D:\Temp2.

   Who is the owner of D:\Temp1\Temp2 and what are the permissions? Why?

   administrator; full control

➤ To move a folder to another NTFS volume

1. Click **Start**, and then click **Run**.
2. In the **Open** box, type **\\student*x*\public** (where **student*x*** is the name of your partner's server) and then click **OK**.

   The Public on Student*x* window appears.
3. Move D:\Temp2 from your computer to \\Student*x*\Public. student10/ full control
4. Click \\Student*x*\Public\Temp2.

   Compare the permissions and ownership of \\Student*x*\Public\Temp2 with the permissions for D:\Temp2 on your computer. What are the similarities and differences?

   similarities / differences;
   full control / ownership

➤ To move a folder within the same NTFS volume

1. Log on as the Sales Manager.
2. Select D:\Temp3 and move the folder structure to D:\Temp1.

   What are the permissions and ownership for D:\Temp1\Temp3? Why?

   Sam Smith (sales manager) full control

➤ **To copy a folder from an NTFS volume to a FAT volume**

1. Copy the D:\Temp1 folder structure to C:\.

   Compare the permissions on C:\Temp1 with the permissions and ownership on D:\Temp1. What are the similarities and differences?

   ____

   ____

2. Exit Windows NT Explorer and log off.

Exercise 3
Identifying Incorrect Permissions

In this exercise, you will identify and solve a common permission-related problem.

Scenario

You are the administrator for a server that contains the folder hierarchy shown in the following illustration.

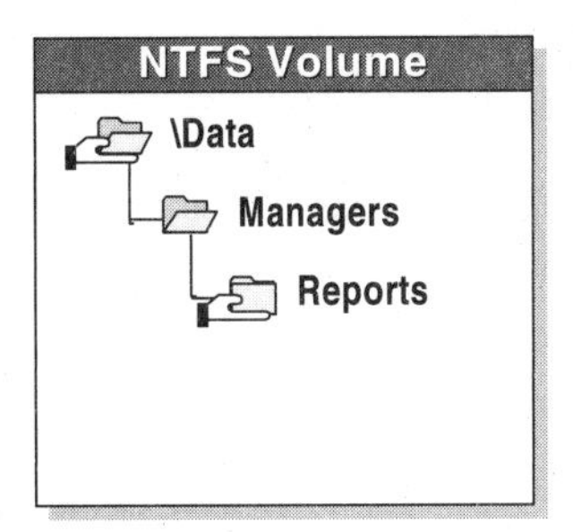

UserA calls you, saying that she does not have proper access to the Reports folder. She is a member of the Managers group.

The following Shared Folder permissions have been assigned:

Folder	Share name	User/group	Shared folder permissions
\Data	Data	Administrators Managers	Full Control Read
\Data\Managers\Reports	Mng_Reports	Administrators Managers	Full Control Full Control

The following NTFS permissions have been assigned:

Folder	User/group	NTFS permissions
\Data	Administrators	Full Control
	Managers	Read
\Managers	Managers	Add & Read
	Creator Owner	Full Control
\Reports	Managers	Add & Read
	Creator Owner	Full Control

When UserA connects to the shared Data folder, she can browse the Managers and Reports folders. She cannot create or modify any files that she owns. What is the problem and how would you solve it?

____

____

Exercise 4
Deleting a File with No Access Permissions

In this exercise, you will observe the result when a user has Full Control permission to a folder and No Access permission to a file in that folder. To do this, you will first assign these permissions.

➤ To assign Full Control access to a folder

1. Log on as Administrator and start Windows NT Explorer.
2. Create a folder on drive D:\ named D:\Fullaccess.
3. Verify that the Everyone group has the Full Control NTFS permission to the folder D:\Fullaccess.

➤ To create and assign No Access to a file

1. Create a text file in the D:\Fullaccess folder named Noaccess.txt.
2. Assign the Everyone group No Access permission for the file Noaccess.txt.

   The following error message appears:

   ```
   You have denied access to D:\Fullaccessl\Noaccess.txt. Nobody will be
   able to access D:\Fullaccess\Noaccess.txt and only the owner will be
   able to change the permissions. Do you wish to continue?
   ```

3. Click **Yes**, and then click **OK**.

➤ **To view the result of Full Control access to a folder**

1. Double-click to open D:\Fullaccess\Noaccess.txt.

   Were you successful? Why or why not?

   ____

   ____

2. Click **Start**, point to **Programs**, and then click **Command Prompt**.
3. Change to D:\Fullaccess.
4. Delete Noaccess.txt.

   very confusing

   Were you successful? Why or why not?

   Yes.

   ____

   How would you prevent users with Full Control permission to a folder from deleting a file in that folder to which they have been assigned the No Access permission?

   ~~put the file~~ give no access perm to everyone

   ____

Exercise 5
Changing Group Membership

In this exercise you will work with a partner to test permissions for a user when that user is connected to a resource. To do this, you will first create a shared folder with permissions.

➤ **To create a shared folder with permissions**

Note Complete this procedure from the PDC.

1. Log on as Administrator.
2. Create a user named UserD.

   What global group is this user automatically a member of?

   domain user

3. From a command prompt, type **net accounts /sync** and press ENTER.

   This command will synchronize the directory databases on the BDC and PDC.

4. Create a folder in the root of drive D named Security.
5. Assign only the NTFS permissions shown in the following table to D:\Security.

Group	NTFS permissions
Users	Read
Administrators	Full Control

6. Share the folder D:\Security as Security, and accept the default permissions: Everyone: Full Control.
7. In the D:\Security folder create a text file named Group.txt.

➤ **To test the shared folder permissions**

Note Wait until the previous procedure has been completed before you begin this procedure. Complete this procedure from the BDC.

1. Log on as UserD.
2. Connect to \\Student*x*\Security (where *x* is your student number) on the PDC.
3. Add some text to Group.txt.

   Were you successful? Why or why not?

   Yes, but cannot save! Read only per

➤ To modify group membership

Note Complete this procedure from the PDC.

- Add UserD to the Domain Admins group.

  What shared folder permissions does UserD have to \\Student*x*\Security on the PDC?

  Full
  ___

  What local permissions does the user have to the folder D:\Security on the PDC?

  ___

➤ To test the new group membership

Note Complete this procedure from the BDC.

1. Add some text to Group.txt.

   Were you successful? Why or why not?

   ___

   ___

2. Log off and then log on as UserD.
3. Add some text to Group.txt.

   Were you successful? Why or Why not?

   ___

   ___

4. Disconnect from the PDC and log off.

Lab 11: Setting Up a Network Printer

Objectives

After completing this lab, you will be able to:

- Add and share a printer.
- Connect to a shared printer.
- Assign printer permissions to users.
- Create a printing pool.
- Schedule documents to print.
- Assign forms to paper trays.
- Set up a separator page.

Estimated time to complete this lab: 45 minutes

Exercise 1
Adding and Sharing a Printer

In this exercise, you will use the Add Printer Wizard to add and share a local printer on your computer.

➤ To add a printer

1. Log on as Administrator.
2. Click **Start**, point to **Settings**, and then click **Printers**.
3. Double-click the Add Printer icon.

   The Add Printer Wizard begins.
4. Click **My Computer**, and then click **Next**.
5. Under **Available Ports**, select the **LPT1** check box, and then click **Next**.
6. Under **Manufacturers**, click **HP**.
7. Under **Printers**, click **HP LaserJet 4Si**, and then click **Next**.

   In the **Printer Name** box, notice Windows NT automatically defaults to the printer name HP LaserJet 4Si.

➤ To share a printer

1. Accept the default printer name by clicking **Next**, and then clicking **Shared**.
2. In the **Share Name** box, type **hplaser4** and then click **Next**.
3. When asked if you want to print a test page, click **No**, and then click **Finish**.

   The **Copying Files—Files Needed** dialog box appears, prompting for the location for the Windows NT Server distribution files.
4. In the **Copy Files From** box, type **\\instructor*x*\winnt** and then click **OK**.

   The printer files are copied.

   The shared printer is created, and an icon for the HP LaserJet 4Si printer appears. Notice that an open hand appears under the printer icon. This signifies that the printer is shared.

➤ **To pause the LaserJet 4Si printer**

1. In the Printers window, double-click the HP LaserJet 4Si icon.

   The HP LaserJet 4Si window appears.

2. On the **Printer** menu, click **Pause Printing**.

Important Pause the printer to prevent it from trying to communicate with a nonexistent print device. This will eliminate error messages in later exercises when documents are processed.

➤ **To print a test document to HP LaserJet 4Si**

1. Click **Start**, point to **Programs**, point to **Accessories**, and then click **Notepad**.
2. In Notepad, type any text you want.
3. Arrange the Notepad window and the HP LaserJet 4Si window so that you can see the contents of each.
4. On the **File** menu, click **Print**.

   You receive a message stating that the document is printing.

   In the HP LaserJet 4Si window, you will see the document waiting to print.

5. Minimize the Notepad and the HP LaserJet 4Si windows.

Exercise 2
Connecting to a Shared Printer

In this exercise, you will use two different methods to connect to a shared printer. First, you will connect to your partner's shared printer, and then you will use a different method to connect to the shared printer on the instructor's computer. You will then set a printer as your default printer and print to it.

Note Pause the printer to prevent it from trying to communicate with a nonexistent print device. This will eliminate error messages in later exercises when documents are processed.

➤ To connect to a shared printer using the Add Printer Wizard

1. In the Printers window, double-click the Add Printer icon.
2. In the **Add Printer Wizard** dialog box, click **Network printer server**, and then click **Next**.

   The **Connect to Printer** dialog box appears.
3. In the **Printer** box, type **\\student*x*\hplaser4** (where **student*x*** is your partner's computer) and then click **OK**.

   Tip You can also double-click **\\student*x*\hplaser4** in the **Shared Printers** list.

   ---

4. When prompted to use the printer as the default printer, click **Next** to accept the default setting of No.

   A message indicates that the network printer has been successfully installed.
5. Click **Finish**.

   The icon for HP LaserJet 4Si on Student*x* appears in the Printers folder. Notice that a network cable appears on the icon for this printer. This indicates that the printer is a network printer.

➤ To connect to the instructor's shared printer using a shortcut

1. On the desktop, double-click Network Neighborhood.

   The Network Neighborhood window appears.
2. Double-click the Entire Network icon.

   The Entire Network window appears.

3. Double-click the Microsoft Windows Network icon.

   The Microsoft Windows Network window appears.

4. Double-click the CLASSROOM*x* domain (where *x* is the number assigned to the Classroom domain).

   All computers in the CLASSROOM*x* domain appear.

5. Double-click Instructor*x* (where *x* is the number assigned to the Instructor computer).

   The available shared resources appear in the Instructor*x* window.

6. Drag the *instructorx_printer* icon to your desktop.

   A **Shortcut** dialog box appears, asking you if you want to create a shortcut.

7. Click **Yes**.

   An icon labeled "Shortcut to *instructorx_printer* on Instructor*x*" appears on your desktop.

8. Close everything except the Printers folder.

➤ To set the default printer

1. In the Printers folder, right-click **HP LaserJet on Student***x* (where *x* is your student number).

2. On the submenu that appears, click **Set As Default**.

   The HP LaserJet on Student*x* printer is now the default printer. Anything you print will go to this printer.

➤ To print a document to the HP LaserJet on Student*x* printer

1. Double-click **HP LaserJet on Student***x* and verify that it is paused.

2. Start Notepad.

3. Arrange the Notepad window and the HP LaserJet 4Si window so that you can see the contents of each.

4. In Notepad, type any text, and then save the file to your desktop as Test.txt.

5. Print the file.

   In the HP LaserJet 4Si on Student*x* window, you will see the document waiting to be printed.

6. Close the **HP LaserJet 4Si on Student***x* dialog box.

7. Close Notepad.

Exercise 3
Assigning Printer Permissions

In this exercise, you will assign printer permissions to the Users group and to two users that you will create. You will also remove the Print permission from the Everyone group to restrict access to only those users you have created.

➤ **To assign permissions to a group**

1. In the Printers folder, click the HP LaserJet 4Si icon, and then, on the **File** menu, click **Properties**.

   The **HP LaserJet 4Si Properties** dialog box appears.

2. Click the **Security** tab, and then click **Permissions**.

   The **Printer Permissions** dialog box appears.

   Which built-in local groups are assigned the Full Control permission by default?

   administrator, print operator, server operator

   Which system groups are assigned the Manage Document permission by default?

   Creator owner

3. Select the Everyone group, and then click **Remove**.
4. Click **Add**.

   The **Add Users and Groups** dialog box appears.

5. Select **Users**, and then click **Add**.

   The Users group appears in the **Add Name** box.

6. In the **Type of Access** box, verify that **Print** is selected, and then click **OK** twice to return to the **HP LaserJet 4Si Properties** dialog box.

➤ **To assign permissions to a user**

1. Create the following user accounts. Substitute your assigned number for *x*:
   - User1-*x*
   - User2-*x*
2. From a command prompt, type **net accounts /sync** and press ENTER to manually synchronize the directory databases.
3. Assign the following permissions to each user:
   - User1-*x*: Manage Documents
   - User2-*x*: Full Control

Exercise 4
Testing Permissions

In this exercise, you will test the permissions for two users by viewing the available printer options for each user.

➤ **To test the Manage Documents permission for User1-*x***

1. Log on as User1-*x* (where *x* is your assigned number).
2. Open the Printers folder.
3. Double-click **Add Printer**.

   What options are available to User1-*x*?

   Network printer server

4. Close the Add Printer window.
5. Click the HP LaserJet 4Si icon, and then on the **File** menu, click **Properties**.
6. Click the **Security** tab, and then click **Permissions**.

   Can you change permissions?

   No

7. Click the **Share** tab.

   Can you share a printer?

   No

8. Click the **Scheduling** tab.

   Can you change printing hours?

   No

9. Click the **Port** tab.

   Can you add ports?

   No

10. Click **Cancel** to close the **HP LaserJet 4Si Properties** dialog box.
11. In the Printers folder, with HP LaserJet 4Si selected, click **File** to view the available menu options, and then click **Purge Print Documents**.

    Can you purge documents from the printer?

    No

➤ To test the Full Control permission for User2-*x*

1. Log on as User2-*x* (where *x* is your assigned number).
2. Try to perform the following tasks. Record the tasks available with the Full Control permission.

   Add a printer__Network__ NO

   Connect to a printer__YES__

   Change a permission__YES__

   Share a printer__YES__

   Schedule a printer__YES__

   Add additional ports__YES__

   Purge a printer__YES__

Exercise 5
Creating a Printer Pool

In this exercise, you will create a printer pool. First, you will pause the printer to prevent it from trying to communicate with a nonexistent print device. This will eliminate error messages in later exercises when documents are spooled.

➤ **To pause the printer**

1. Log on as Administrator.
2. Click **Start**, point to **Settings**, and then click **Printers**.
3. In the Printers window, double-click the HP LaserJet 4Si icon.

   The HP LaserJet 4Si window appears.
4. On the **Printer** menu, verify that **Pause Printing** is selected.
5. Close the HP LaserJet 4Si window.

➤ **To create a printer pool**

1. In the Printers window, select the HP LaserJet 4Si icon.
2. On the **File** menu, click **Properties**.

   The **HP LaserJet 4Si Properties** dialog box appears.
3. Click the **Ports** tab.

   The **Ports** tab appears, and **LPT1** is selected.
4. Select **Enable printer pooling**.
5. Click **COM2,** and then click **LPT2**.

   For this exercise, in what order will the printer check for available ports?

   LPT2, COM2
   ___
6. Click **OK**.

Exercise 6
Scheduling Documents to Print

In this exercise, you will schedule documents to print by setting the printer priority and available printer hours.

➤ To set a printer priority

1. Make sure the Printers window is active and that the HP LaserJet 4Si icon is selected.
2. On the **File** menu, click **Properties**.

   The **HP LaserJet 4Si Properties** dialog box appears.

   Note You can also right-click the HP LaserJet 4Si icon, and then click **Properties** to access the **HP LaserJet 4Si Properties** dialog box.

   ---

3. Click the **Scheduling** tab.

   What is the default priority for a printer?

   available always
4. In the **Priority** section, move the slider to the highest priority.

   What is that priority?

   a lowest 1

➤ To set available printing hours

1. Make sure that the **Scheduling** tab is active.

   What is the default setting for available printing hours?

   ~~12:00 am → 12:00 am~~ always
2. Click **From**.
3. Set the available printer hours from 8:00 P.M. until 8:00 A.M.
4. Click **OK**.

➤ **To test the available printing hours**

1. Double-click the HP LaserJet 4Si icon.

   The **HP LaserJet 4Si** dialog box appears.

2. On the Printer menu, click **Set As Default Printer**.

3. On the **Printer** menu, click **Pause Printing**.

   Notice that on the **Printer** menu, the check mark next to **Pause Printing** disappears.

4. Open the Text.txt file that you created previously using Notepad.

   Arrange the Notepad window and the HP LaserJet 4Si window on your desktop so you can see both.

5. Print Test.txt.

   Look at the status of the files to be printed in the HP LaserJet 4Si window.

   Notice that the status of the document is not "Printing" or "Paused." This indicates that the document is not attempting to print.

6. Minimize Notepad.

Exercise 7
Assigning Forms to Paper Trays

In this exercise, you will assign a paper type (form) to a paper tray so that when users print to a specified form, the print job will automatically be routed to and adjusted for the correct tray.

➤ **To assign forms to paper trays**

1. Verify that the HP LaserJet 4Si window is active.
2. On the **Printer** menu, click **Properties**.

   The **HP LaserJet 4Si Properties** dialog box appears.
3. Click the **Device Settings** tab.

   Notice that there are multiple selections under **Form to Tray Assignment**, and that most of them are labeled <Not Available>. This is because no specific tray assignments have been configured.
4. Click **Upper Paper Tray**.
5. In the **Change 'Upper Paper Tray' Setting** box, click **Letter Small**.

   Notice that **Upper Paper Tray** is now available.
6. Assign **Envelope #10** to the **Envelope Feeder**.
7. Click **OK**.

Exercise 8
Setting Up Separator Pages

In this exercise, you will set up a separator page to print between documents. This separator page will include the user's name and the date and time the document was printed.

➤ **To set up a separator page**

1. Verify that the **HP LaserJet 4Si** dialog box is active.
2. On the **Printer** menu, click **Properties**.

   The **HP LaserJet 4Si Properties** dialog box appears with the **General** tab active.
3. On the **General** tab, click **Separator Page**.

   The **Separator Page** dialog box appears.
4. Click **Browse**.

   Another **Separator Page** dialog box appears.

   What are the three separator page files that you can select?

   ____

   ____
5. Select Sysprint.sep, and then click **Open**.

   The first **Separator Page** dialog box appears.
6. Click **OK**.

   The **HP LaserJet 4Si Properties** dialog box appears with the **General** tab active.
7. On the **General** tab, click **OK**.

Lab 12: Managing Documents and Printers

Objectives

After completing this lab, you will be able to:

- Set a notification for a document.
- Change the priority of a document.
- Cancel a document.
- Redirect documents to another printer.
- Purge a printer.
- Take ownership of a printer.

Before You Begin

Prerequisites

This lab assumes that you installed an HP LaserJet 4Si printer. If your server does not have this configuration, see Lab 11: Setting Up a Network Printer.

It also assumes that an account named User2-*x* (where *x* is your assigned number) exists in the domain with the Full Control print permission for the printer. If this user account with this permission does not exist, create it now.

Estimated time to complete this lab: 15 minutes

Exercise 1
Managing Documents

In this exercise, you will practice managing documents by pausing and resuming the printing of a document, canceling a document, setting a notification, and changing a document priority.

Important Keep the printer paused to prevent it from trying to communicate with a nonexistent print device. This will eliminate error messages in later exercises when documents are spooled.

➤ **To pause the printer**

1. Log on as Administrator.
2. Open the Printers window, and then double-click the HP LaserJet 4Si icon.

   The **HP LaserJet 4Si** dialog box appears.
3. On the **Printer** menu, click **Pause Printing**.

➤ **To print documents**

1. Locate and select the Notepad documents **Hamlet.txt** and **Bronte.txt** in the D:\LabFiles\Public\Library folder.
2. Right-click the selected documents, and on the shortcut menu that appears, click **Print**.

➤ **To set a notification**

1. In the HP LaserJet 4Si Printer window, select **Bronte.txt**.
2. On the **Document** menu, click **Properties**.

   The **General** tab of the **Bronte.txt Properties** dialog box appears.
3. In the **Notify** box, type **User2-*x***

➤ To increase the document priority

1. On the **General** tab of the **Bronte.txt Properties** dialog box, notice the default priority.

   What is the default priority? Is it the lowest or highest priority?

   1 / 99

2. On the **General** tab, use the slider to increase the priority of the document.
3. Click **OK**.

   Nothing changes visibly in the HP LaserJet 4Si Printer window, but the document prints before other documents.

➤ To cancel a document

1. In the HP LaserJet 4Si Printer window, select **Hamlet.txt**.
2. On the **Document** menu, click **Cancel**.

   How can you tell that the document is canceled?

   ____

Exercise 2
Managing Printers

In this exercise, you will perform tasks to manage printers. These tasks include redirecting documents, taking ownership of a printer, and purging a printer.

Note Before you begin, make sure that the HP LaserJet 4Si printer is paused and that there are documents in the print queue.

➤ To redirect documents to another printer

1. In the HP LaserJet 4Si Printer window, on the **Printer** menu, click **Properties**.

   The **HP LaserJet 4Si Properties** dialog box appears.
2. Click the **Ports** tab, and then click **Add Port**.

   The **Printer Ports** dialog box appears.
3. Click **Local Port**, and then click **New Port**.

   The **Port Name** dialog box appears.
4. In the **Enter a Port Name** box, type **\\student*x*\hplaser4** (where **student*x*** is the name of your partner's computer).
5. Click **OK**, and then click **Close**.

   How can you tell that the port has been added?

   \\student 10\hplaser 4 checked
   ____

   How would you make sure that the documents in your print queue would redirect to \\student*x*\hplaser4? x

   ____
6. Click **OK**.

➤ To purge a printer

1. Verify that the **HP LaserJet 4Si** dialog box is active.
2. On the **Printer** menu, click **Purge Print Documents**.

   How can you tell if the documents are purged?

   ____
3. Close the HP LaserJet 4Si Printer window and log off.

➤ **To take ownership of a printer**

1. Log on as User2-*x*.
2. Open the Printers window, and then double-click the HP LaserJet 4Si icon.

   The HP LaserJet 4Si window appears.
3. On the **Printer** menu, click **Properties**.

   The **HP LaserJet 4Si Properties** dialog box appears.
4. Click the **Security** tab, and then click **Ownership**.

   Who currently owns the printer?

   administrator
   ___
5. Attempt to take ownership of the printer.

   Were you able to take ownership? Why or why not?

   No
   ___

   ___

Tip Check the permissions that have been assigned to User2-*x* for the printer.

Lab 13: Auditing Resources and Events

Objectives

After completing this lab, you will be able to:

- Plan an audit policy for the domain.
- Set up the audit policy.
- Set up auditing on a file.
- Set up auditing on a printer.
- Locate and view events in the security log.
- Archive the security log.
- Clear the security log.
- View events in the archived security log.

Before You Begin

Prerequisites

This lab assumes that you have a printer installed named HPLaser4. If you have not installed a printer, see Lab 11: Setting Up a Network Printer.

Estimated time to complete this lab: 30 minutes

Exercise 1
Planning a Domain Audit Policy

In this exercise, you will plan an audit policy for the Quebec domain. You need to determine:

- Which types of events to audit.
- Whether to audit the success or failure of an event, or both.

Use the following criteria to make your decisions:

- Record unsuccessful attempts to access the network.
- Record unauthorized access to the AR, HR, and customer databases.
- For billing purposes, track color printer usage.
- Track any time someone tries to tamper with the server hardware.
- Keep a record of actions performed by an administrator to track unauthorized changes.
- Track backup procedures to prevent data theft.

Record your decisions on the following graphic.

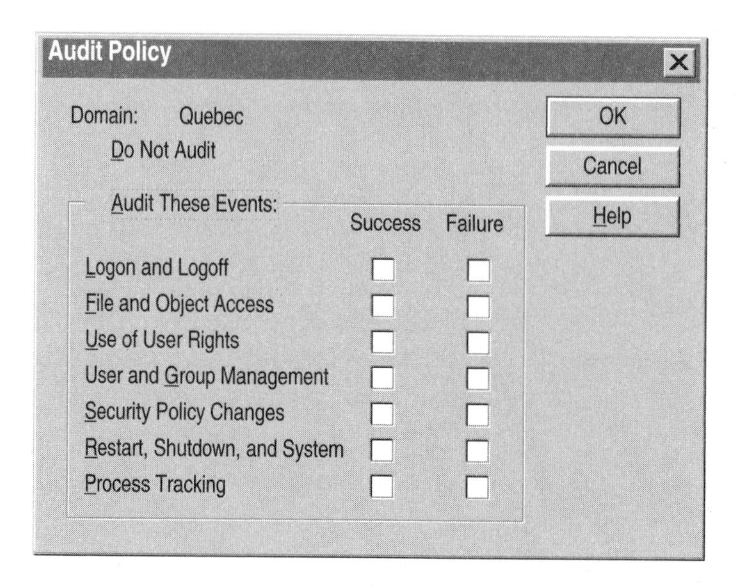

Exercise 2
Setting Up an Audit Policy

In this exercise, you will enable auditing for selected events.

➤ **To set up the audit policy**

Note Because there can only be one audit policy for a domain, complete this procedure on the PDC only.

---

1. Log on as Administrator.
2. Start User Manager for Domains.
3. On the **Policies** menu, click **Audit**.

   The **Audit Policy** dialog box appears.
4. Click **Audit These Events**.
5. Set the audit policy by selecting either the **Success** or **Failure** check box for the events that you identified in the planning exercise.
6. Click **OK**.

Exercise 3
Auditing Files and Directories

In this exercise, you will set up auditing for a file.

➤ **To set up file auditing**

1. Start Windows NT Explorer and expand drive D.
2. In the \LabFiles\Public\Library directory, right-click **Bronte.txt**.
3. Click **Properties**, and then click the **Security** tab.

> **Tip** Auditing can only be done on NTFS partitions. If the **Security** tab does not appear, it indicates that the selected file is not on an NTFS partition.

4. Click **Auditing**.

   The **File Auditing** dialog box appears.
5. Click **Add**.

   The **Add User and Groups** dialog box appears.
6. In the **Names** list, click **Everyone**, and then click **Add**.
7. Click **OK**.

   The Everyone group appears in the **File Auditing** dialog box.
8. Under **Events to Audit**, select the **Success** check box for the following events:
   - **Delete**
   - **Change Permission**
   - **Take Ownership**
9. Click **OK** to apply your changes.
10. Click **OK** to exit the **Properties** dialog box and return to Windows NT Explorer.

Exercise 4
Auditing a Printer

In this exercise, you will set up auditing for a printer.

➤ **To audit a printer**

1. Click **Start**, point to **Settings**, and then click **Printers**.
2. In the Printers window, double-click the printer **HP LaserJet 4Si**.
3. On the **Printer** menu, click **Properties**.
4. Click the **Security** tab.
5. Click **Auditing**.

   The **Printer Auditing** dialog box appears.
6. Click **Add**.
7. In the **Names** list, click **Everyone**, and then click **Add**.
8. Click **OK**.
9. Under **Events to Audit**, select the **Success** check box for the following events:
   - **Print**
   - **Change Permissions**
   - **Take Ownership**
10. Click **OK** to apply your changes.
11. Click **OK** to close the **HP LaserJet 4Si Properties** dialog box.
12. Close the Printer window.

Exercise 5
Creating Security Log Entries

In this exercise, you will perform tasks that create entries in the security log so that you can view the entries.

➤ **To create log file entries**

1. Log off and then log on as any user.
2. Connect to \\Student*x*\Public (where Student*x* is your partner's computer).
3. Open the file **\Library\Bronte.txt** by double-clicking it.
4. Close the file.
5. Log off and then log on as Administrator.
6. Create a user account.
7. Shut down and restart your computer.

Exercise 6
Viewing the Security Log

In this exercise, you will view the security log for your computer and for another computer.

➤ **To view the security log for your computer**

1. Log on as Administrator.
2. In **Administrative Tools**, click **Event Viewer**.

   The system log for your computer appears.
3. On the **Log** menu, click **Security**.
4. Scroll through the log and look for the following categories of events.
   - **Logon/Logoff**
   - **Object Access**
   - **Privilege Use**
   - **Account Manager**
5. Double-click the different events for a description of them.

➤ **To view the security log for another computer**

1. On the **Log** menu, click **Select Computer**.

   The **Select Computer** dialog box appears.

2. In the **Computer** box, type **student***x* (where **student***x* is your partner's computer) and then click **OK**.

   The Event Viewer for your partner's computer appears.

3. If the Security log does not already appear, on the **Log menu**, click **Security**.

4. Scroll through the log and look for the following categories of events.

   - **Logon/Logoff**
   - **Object Access**
   - **Privilege Use**
   - **Account Manager**

5. Double-click the different events for a description of them.

   Notice that you can view all security events for the remote computer.

6. On the **Log** menu, click **Select Computer**.

   The **Select Computer** dialog box appears.

7. In the **Computer** box, type **student***x* (where **student***x* is your computer) and then click **OK**.

Exercise 7
Filtering and Searching Events

In this exercise, you will use Event Viewer to filter events and to search for potential security breaches.

➤ **To filter for Logon/Logoff events**

1. In Event Viewer, on the **Log** menu, click **Open**.

   The **Open** dialog box appears.

2. Open the Security.evt file in the D:\LabFiles folder.

   The **Open File Type** dialog box appears. The System file type is selected by default.

3. Under **Open File of Type**, click **Security**, and then click **OK**.

   The Security event log for Security.evt appears.

4. On the **View** menu, click **Filter Events**.

   The **Filter** dialog box appears.

5. In the **Source** box, click **Security**.
6. In the **Category** box, click **Logon/Logoff**, and then click **OK**.
7. Double-click each event for a description.

   What types of Logon/Logoff events were recorded that may indicate someone was attempting to access the system?

   ____

➤ **To filter for unauthorized access to files and folders events**

1. On the **View** menu, click **Filter Events**.

   The **Filter** dialog box appears.

2. In the **Source** box, click **Security**.
3. In the **Category** box, click **Object Access**.
4. Under **Types**, select the **Failure Audit** check box, and then click to clear all other check boxes.
5. Click **OK**.

6. Double-click each event to see a description.

   What file could not be accessed? (If necessary, scroll through the list.)

   ___

   What action was attempted on the file?

   delete

➤ To search for printer usage events using the Find command

1. On the **View** menu, click **All Events**.
2. On the **View** menu, click **Find**.

   The **Find** dialog box appears.
3. In the **Description** box, type **printer** and then click **Find Next**.

   The first event containing the found text will be highlighted.
4. On the **View** menu, click **Detail**.

   In the **Description** box, under **Accesses**, what action was performed?

   read control

➤ To search for server hardware events using the Find command

1. On the **View** menu, click **Find**.

   The **Find** dialog box appears.
2. Click **Clear** to reset the **Find** dialog box options.
3. In the **Description** box, type **shutdown** and then click **Find Next**.

   The first event containing the found text will be highlighted.
4. On the **View** menu, click **Detail**.

   When was the last time the computer was shut down?

   ___

➤ To reset Event Viewer to view logs on your own computer

1. On the **Log** menu, click **Select Computer**.

   The **Select Computer** dialog box appears.
2. In the **Computer** box, type **student***x* (where **student***x* is your computer) and then click **OK**.

Exercise 8
Controlling the Security Log

In this exercise, you will configure Event Viewer to overwrite events when the log file gets full.

➤ **To control the size and contents of a log file**

1. On the **Log** menu, click **Log Settings**.

   The **Event Log Settings** dialog box appears.

2. Select **Overwrite Events as Needed**.

   Older events will now be overwritten by new events.

3. Click **OK** when finished.

Exercise 9
Archiving the Security Log

In this exercise, you will archive the current security log.

➤ **To archive the security log**

1. Start Windows NT Explorer and expand drive D.
2. Create a folder named Archives in D:\.
3. Exit Windows NT Explorer, and then go to Event Viewer.
4. On the **Log** menu, click **Security**.
5. On the **Log** menu, click **Save As**.
6. In the **File Name** box, type a name that easily identifies the file.

Tip If you archive security logs, include the date as part of the file name to help you locate the file quickly.

---

7. In the **Save in** box, click **(D:)**, double-click the **\Archives** folder, and click **Save**.

Exercise 10
Clearing the Security Log

In this exercise, you will clear the security log.

➤ **To clear the security log**

1. On the **Log** menu, click **Clear All Events**.

   A message appears, asking you if you want to save the event log before closing it.

2. Click **No**.

   Another message appears, warning that this is an irreversible action and requesting verification.

3. Click **Yes**.

   Do any events appear in the security log?

   Yes
   ____

   What is the description of this event?

   ____

Exercise 11
Viewing an Archived Security Log

In this exercise, you will view an archived security log.

➤ **To view an archived security log**

1. On the **Log** menu, click **Open**.
2. In the **File Name** box, type the path and name of the file that you archived or, in the **Look in** list, select the file.
3. Click **Open**.
4. In the **Files of type** box, click **Security**.
5. Click **OK**.
6. Exit Event Viewer.

Lab 14: Monitoring Network Resources

Objectives

After completing this lab, you will be able to:

- Add a user to the Server Operators group.
- Determine the built-in rights of the Server Operators group.
- View open files.
- View a list of all users connected to the server.
- View a list of resources shared by computers.
- View a list of open resources on the server.
- Send a message to a connected user.
- Observe the effects of disconnecting remote users.

Estimated time to complete this lab: 30 minutes

Exercise 1
Adding a User to the Server Operators Group

In this exercise, you will give a user the rights to administer the server by adding their account to the Server Operators group.

➤ To add a user to the Server Operators group

1. Log on as Administrator and start User Manager for Domains.
2. Create a user account and add it to the Server Operators group.
3. From a command prompt, type **net accounts /sync** and press ENTER to make the account available throughout the domain immediately.

➤ To determine the built-in rights that are assigned to Server Operators

1. In the User Manager for Domains window, on the **Policies** menu, click **User Rights**.
2. Select each user right to determine which of them are assigned to the Server Operators group by default. Select the appropriate boxes.

   Access this computer from network

   Add workstations to domain

   Back up files and directories ✓

   Change the system time ✓

   Force shutdown from a remote system ✓

   Load and unload device drivers

   Log on locally ✓

   Manage auditing and security log

   Restore files and directories ✓

   Shut down the system ✓

   Take ownership of files or other objects
3. Exit User Manager for Domains and log off Windows NT.

Exercise 2
Viewing Open Files and User Sessions and Connections

In this exercise, you will use Server Manager to view open files, user sessions, and user connections to your server.

➤ **To open a remote resource**

1. Log on to your computer using the account that you created and added to the Server Operators group in the previous exercise.
2. Right-click Network Neighborhood, and click **Map Network Drive**.

   The **Map Network Drive** dialog box appears.
3. Connect drive P to the Public shared folder on your partner's computer.
4. Start WordPad (from the **Accessories** menu) and open P:\Expenses.doc.
5. Minimize Word Viewer.

➤ **To view open files**

Note Make sure your partner has completed the previous procedure before you continue.

---

1. In Administrative Tools, start Server Manager, and then double-click the name of your server.

   The **Properties for Student***x* dialog box appears.
2. Click **In Use**.

   The **Open Resources on Student***x* dialog box appears.

   What resources are currently open?

   ____

   Who is using the open files?

   ____

   For what tasks have the files been opened?

   ____
3. Click **Close** to return to the **Properties for Student***x* dialog box.

➤ **To view existing sessions and connections**

1. In the **Properties for Student***x* dialog box, click **Users**.

   The **User Sessions on Student***x* dialog box appears.

   Notice the users that have established a session with your server.

   Notice the connections that have been established to your server.

2. Click **Start**, and then click **Run**.
3. In the **Run** box, type **\\student***x***\netlogon** (where **student***x* is your partner's computer) and then click **OK**.

   A Windows NT Explorer window that shows the contents of the Users shared folder appears.

4. Switch to Server Manager.
5. Update the contents of the **User Sessions on Student***x* dialog box by closing the dialog box and then opening it.

   Notice the resources in use.

6. Click **Close** to return to the **Properties for Student***x* dialog box.

Exercise 3
Viewing Server Resource Usage

In this exercise, you will use Server Manager to view resources shared by other computers, to view which resources are open on the server, and to create a shared folder.

➤ To view a list of resources shared by computers

Note Complete this procedure while logged on as the user account that you added to the Server Operators group in Exercise 1.

---

1. In the **Properties for Student*x*** dialog box, click **Shares**.

   The **Shared Resources on Student*x*** dialog box appears.

2. Under **Sharename**, click **Public**.

   Who is connected to the Public share?

   No
   ___

   Is anyone connected to the IPC$ share? If so, who?

   Yes' Student 10
   ___

3. Click **Close** to return to the **Properties for Student*x*** dialog box.

➤ To view a list of open resources on the server

1. In the **Properties for Student*x*** dialog box, click **In Use**.

   Notice the resources in use on Student*x*.

2. Click **Close** to return to the **Properties for Student*x*** dialog box.

➤ To set an administrative alert

1. Log on as Administrator, start Server Manager, and then double-click the name of your server.
2. Click **Alerts**.

   The **Alerts on Student*x*** dialog box appears.

3. In the **New Computer or Username** box, type **Administrator** and click **Add**.

   Administrator appears under **Send Administrative Alerts To**.

4. Click **OK** twice to apply your changes.
5. Exit all applications and log off Windows NT.

Exercise 4
Disconnecting a User

In this exercise, you will work with your partner. You will send a message to the user at the BDC and use the PDC to disconnect that user from a shared resource.

➤ **To connect to a shared resource**

Note Complete this procedure from the BDC.

---

1. Log on using the account that you created for your Server Operators group in Exercise 1.
2. Connect to the Public shared folder on the PDC.
3. Use Notepad to create a text file and save it in the Public folder.

   Do not close the file.

➤ **To send a message to users connected to a server**

Note Complete this procedure from the PDC.

---

1. Log on using the account that you created for your Server Operators group in Exercise 1.
2. Start Server Manager, and then click the PDC icon.
3. On the **Computer** menu, click **Send Message**.

   The **Send Message** dialog box appears.
4. Under **Message**, type a message notifying users to save any open files and that they are about to be disconnected.
5. Click **OK** to send the message.

   What computer or computers received the message?

   Student09/10
   ____

   What information was added to your message?

   Message f
   ____

➤ To disconnect a user from a shared resource

Note Complete this procedure from the PDC.

---

1. In Server Manager, make sure that the PDC is selected.
2. On the **Computer** menu, click **Properties**.

   The **Properties for Student***x* dialog box appears.
3. Click **Users**.

   The **User Sessions on Student***x* dialog box appears.
4. Click **Disconnect All**.

   A Server Manager message box appears, warning you that disconnecting users may cause loss of data.
5. Click **Yes** to disconnect the users.

   What happened in the **User Sessions on Student***x* dialog box when the user was disconnected?

   Blank
   ____

➤ To observe the effect of disconnecting a user

Note Complete this procedure from the BDC.

---

1. Did you notice any changes on your computer when you were disconnected from the PDC?

   ____
2. In the text file you created, add more text, and then save the file.

   Did you need to reconnect to the Public folder on the PDC to save the file? Why or why not?

   ____
3. Exit all applications and log off Windows NT.

Exercise 5 *(optional)*
Creating a Shared Folder on a Remote Server

In this exercise, you will use Server Manager to share a folder on your partner's computer.

➤ **To create a shared folder on a remote server**

1. Log on as Administrator and start Server Manager.
2. Select your partner's computer, and then, on the **Computer** menu, click **Shared Directories**.

   The **Shared Directories** dialog box appears.
3. Select the **ADMIN$** shared folder, and then click **Properties**.

   Notice that the Comment for the ADMIN$ share indicates that it is used for remote administration.
4. Click **Cancel** to return to the **Shared Directories** dialog box.
5. Click **New Share**.

   The **New Share** dialog box appears.
6. In the **Share Name** box, type **Library***x* (where *x* is your student number).
7. In the **Path** box, type **d:\labfiles\public\library** and then click **OK** to apply your changes.

   The **Shared Directories** dialog box appears.
8. Click **Close**.
9. Exit all applications and log off Windows NT.

Exercise 6 *(optional)*
Using Windows NT Diagnostics to View Configuration Information

In this exercise, you will use Windows NT Diagnostics to view configuration information.

➤ **To view software configuration information**

1. Log on as Administrator.
2. In Administrative Tools, start Windows NT Diagnostics.
3. Locate and record the following information by reviewing each tab.

Requested information	WinMSD tab	Value
Registered owner		
Registered organization		
Version number		
Build number		
System root (windir)		
Domain name		
CPU type		

4. Locate and record the following information.

Requested information	Your configuration
Total physical memory	
Available physical memory	
Total page file space	
Available page file space	
Paging files	

Lab 15: Backing Up Data to Tape

Objectives

After completing this lab, you will be able to:

- Plan a backup schedule.
- Grant a user only the right to back up files to tape.
- Back up files to tape.
- Write a batch file to back up files and folders.
- Schedule the Backup program to start automatically.

Estimated time to complete this lab: 45 minutes

Exercise 1
Planning a Backup Schedule

In this exercise, you will work with your partner to plan a backup schedule for the following data. Record your decisions on the *Backup Planning Worksheet*.

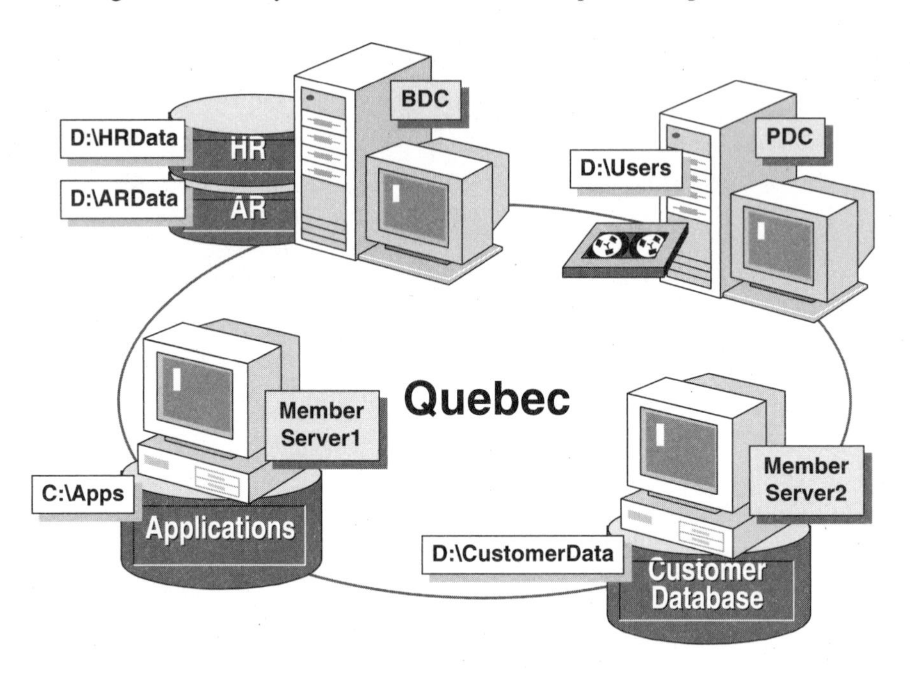

You need to determine:

- Whether files and folders should be backed up daily or weekly.
- A weekly backup schedule that includes a backup type for each day, which tape to use, and whether that tape will be archived or reused.

Use the following criteria to make your decisions:

- Applications are upgraded approximately every three months. Minor updates are applied as necessary.
- The Accounts Receivable (AR) database is updated each day with full and partial payments received from customers.
- The Human Resources (HR) database is updated every time a new employee is hired or an existing employee goes on vacation.
- Users store letters, memos, and archived e-mail in their home folders. Most data does not change frequently.
- Critical customer files are stored in the Customer database.
- Lost data must be restorable in a quick and easy manner.
- All backups should be well documented.

Exercise 2
Adding a User to the Backup Operators Group

In this exercise, you will remove the **Restore files and directories** user right from the Backup Operators group and then give a user the rights to back up the computer by adding their account to a global group and assigning the global group membership in the Backup Operators group.

Note Complete the following procedure from the PDC only.

➤ **To restrict Backup Operators from restoring files and directories**

1. Log on as Administrator and start User Manager for Domains.
2. On the **Policies** menu, click **User Rights**.

   The **User Rights Policy** dialog box appears.
3. In the **Right** box, click **Restore files and directories**.
4. In the **Grant To** box, click **Backup Operators**, and then click **Remove**.
5. Click **OK** to apply your changes.
6. Create a global group named *Backup Only*.
7. Add the Backup Only group to the Backup Operators group.

➤ **To give a user the rights to back up the computer**

Note Complete this procedure from both computers.

---

1. Create a user account.
2. Add the user to the Backup Only group.
3. Close User Manager for Domains.
4. From a command prompt, type **net accounts /sync** and press ENTER to make the account available throughout the domain immediately.

Exercise 3
Backing Up Files to Tape

In this exercise, you will use the Backup Simulation program to simulate backing up files to tape. This simulation will include:

- Erasing the tape.
- Selecting files and folders to back up.
- Selecting the backup type.
- Selecting backup and log options.

Note The Backup Simulation program allows you to perform a backup without having a tape drive connected to your computer.

➤ **To start the Backup Simulation program**

1. While logged on as Administrator, click **Start**, point to **Programs**, and then click **Backup Simulation**.
2. The Backup Simulation window appears.

➤ **To erase a tape**

1. In the Backup Simulation window, on the **Operations** menu, click **Erase Tape**.

   The **Erase Tape** dialog box appears.
2. Click **Secure Erase**, and then click **Continue**.

   The Erase Status window appears.
3. When the tape is erased, click **OK**.

➤ **To select files and folders to be backed up**

1. Double-click the disk icon for drive D.

   The D:*.* window appears.

2. Expand the folder hierarchy for drive D.
3. Select only the check boxes of the following files and folders:
   - D:\Data\Managers\Sven.doc
   - D:\Public\Library\Bronte*.*
   - D:\Public\Templates\Time*.*

Note If you were using Windows NT Backup, the check box for the parent folder of the selected file would appear dimmed. The Backup Simulation program does not do this.

➤ **To begin the backup process**

1. In the Backup Simulation window, click **Backup**.

   –or–

   On the **Operations** menu, click **Backup**.

   The **Backup Information** dialog box appears.

2. If you want a tape name other than the default, in the **Tape Name** box, type a descriptive name for your tape. For example, **Archive data** *today's date*
3. Select the following options:
   - **Replace**
   - **Verify After Backup**
   - **Restrict Access To Owner or Administrator**

   Why is the **Append** option unavailable?

   ____

➤ To specify a backup set description

1. In the **Description** box, type a descriptive name for your backup. For example, type **Classics** *today's date*
2. In the **Backup Type** box, click **Normal**.
3. Accept the default path of D:\Winnt\Backup.log for the log file.
4. In the **Log Information** box, click **Full Detail**, and then click **OK.**

   The Backup Status window appears.
5. When the backup process is finished, click **OK**.

   The Tapes window appears.
6. Minimize the Backup Simulation window.

Important The Backup Simulation program is designed to back up and restore files in a single operation. This means that if you close the program, you will need to perform another backup before you are able to restore files in Lab 16.

➤ To view the backup log

1. Start Windows NT Explorer.
2. Open the Backup.log file located in the D:\Winnt folder.

   Look at the file. What files were backed up in the Template folder?

   ____
3. Close the backup log.

Note The Backup Simulation program will only create a Full Detail log.

Exercise 4
Writing a Batch File to Back Up Data

In this exercise, you will work with your partner to write a batch file to schedule a backup for servers in the Quebec domain.

The batch file should:

- Back up the files in both the shared CustomerData folder and the shared ARData folder that have changed since the last backup markers were set. Do not set new backup markers.
- Back up the Registry.
- Provide the description "Customer Data" on the backup tape.
- Create a log named Tuesday.log
- Verify the backup.
- Add the backup to the Tuesday backup tape.
- Not implement hardware compression.

The following are the network servers and the data that they contain.

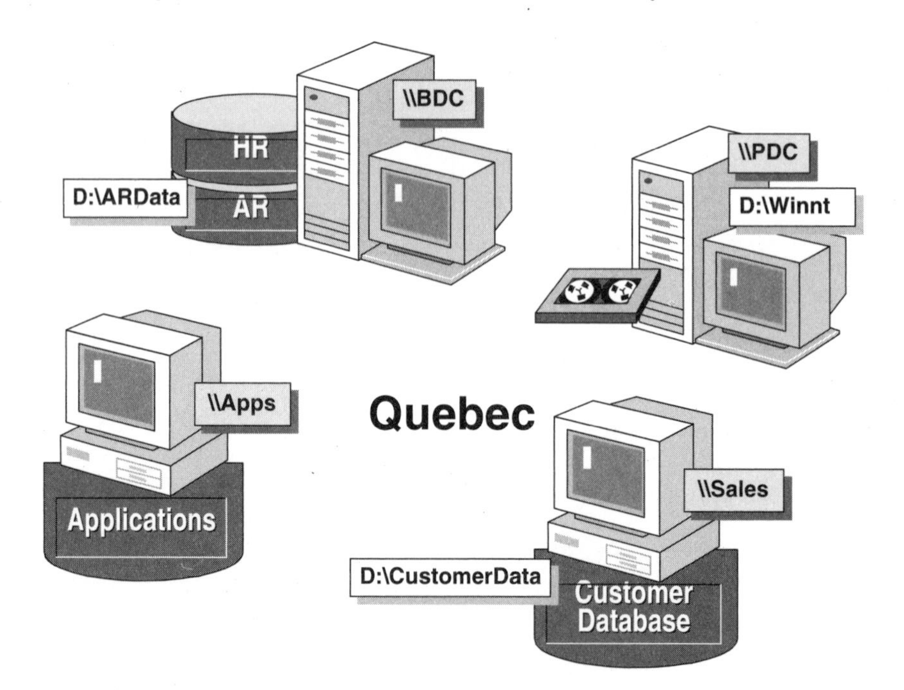

➤ To plan a batch file

- Write down the commands that should appear in the batch file. Use the following command options.

Option	Description
/A	Appends the backup set.
/B	Backs up the local Registry.
/D "*text*"	Describes the backup set.
/E	Logs exceptions, such as summary log, or don't log. If this option is not used, a full detail log is created.
/L *file name*	Assigns a file name to the log file.
/R	Limits access to the tape to Administrators, Backup Operators, or the user who performed the backup.
/T {Normal I Copy I Incremental I Differential I Daily}	Specifies the backup type.
/V	Confirms that the files were backed up accurately.
/HC:{ON IOFF}	Enables or disables hardware compression for tape drives that support it.
cmd /c net use *x:*	Connects to a remote share.
cmd /c net use *x*: **/delete**	Disconnects from a remote share.

____

____

____

Exercise 5
Scheduling the Backup

In this exercise, you will schedule unattended events to run on your computer and on a remote computer. You will schedule Notepad and Solitaire instead of the Backup program because your computer does not have a tape drive.

Note Before you can use the **at** command, the Windows NT Schedule service must be running. In this exercise, you will start the Schedule service to start automatically when the computer is restarted.

➤ **To start the Schedule service**

1. Start Server Manager.

   The Server Manager window appears.
2. Select your computer, and then, on the **Computer** menu, click **Services**.

   The **Services on** *server_name* dialog box appears.
3. In the **Service** box, click **Schedule**, and then click **Startup**.

   The **Service on** *server_name* dialog box appears.
4. In the **Startup Type** box, click **Automatic**, and then click **OK**.
5. In the **Services on** *server_name* dialog box, click **Start**.

   The Schedule service starts.
6. In the Services window, click **Close**.
7. Exit Server Manager.

➤ To configure the Schedule service using the at command

1. Start a command prompt.
2. Check the **at** command syntax by typing **help at|more** and then pressing ENTER.
3. Read the information about the **at** command.
4. Check the current system time and write it down here:

   ____

5. Add two minutes to the system time, type the following command, and then press ENTER. Substitute the future time for *hh:mm* using the 24-hour format.

   at *hh:mm* **/interactive "d:\winnt\system32\notepad.exe"**

   Notepad should run on your computer within the next couple of minutes.

Note If Notepad fails to run, use the taskbar clock to verify that the time that you entered is correct for A.M. or P.M.

➤ To configure the at command to schedule events for a remote computer

---

Note Make sure that your partner has completed the previous procedure and that the Schedule service has started before you begin this procedure.

---

1. Ask your partner for the current system time of his or her computer and write it down here:

   ____

2. Add two minutes to the system time, type the following command, and then press ENTER. Substitute the future time for *hh:mm.*

   at ***partner's_server hh:mm* **/i "d:\winnt\system32\sol.exe"

   Solitaire should run on your partner's computer within the next couple of minutes.

   Note If Notepad fails to run, use the taskbar clock to verify that the time that you entered is correct for A.M. or P.M.

   ---

3. Close the command prompt window.

Exercise 6 *(optional)*
Using the Command Scheduler

In this exercise you will use the Resource Kit tool Command Scheduler to configure the Windows NT Schedule service and start Freecell at a specified time. This tool has been added to your **Program** menu.

➤ **To configure the Schedule service using Command Scheduler**

1. Click **Start**, point to **Programs**, and then click **Command Scheduler**.

   The Command Scheduler window appears.

   Note If the Schedule service is not running on your server, Command Scheduler will prompt you to start it.

   ---

2. Click **Add**.

   The **Add Command** dialog box appears.

3. In the **Command** box, type **d:\winnt\system32\freecell.exe**
4. Under **This Occurs**, click **Today**.

   Under **Days**, notice that the current day is selected.

5. Under **Time**, add two minutes to the system time to specify a future time.
6. Select **Interactive**, and then click **OK**.

   Notice that the configured command appears in the Command Scheduler window.

7. Exit Command Scheduler and wait until the entered time arrives.

   Freecell should run on your computer within the next couple of minutes.

Lab 16: Restoring Data from Tape

Objectives

After completing this lab, you will be able to:

- Implement a restore strategy.
- Grant a user only the right to restore files.
- Restore files and directories from a tape.

Before You Begin

Prerequisites

This lab assumes that you have successfully completed a backup operation using the Backup Simulation program in Lab 15: Backing Up Data to Tape. It is also assumed that you minimized, but did not close, the Backup Simulation program.

If you closed the Backup Simulation program, repeat Lab 15 now.

Estimated time to complete this lab: 30 minutes

Exercise 1
Implementing a Restore Strategy

In this exercise, you will determine a restore strategy based on how the corrupted data was backed up as provided in the scenario.

Scenario

Your backups had the following characteristics:

- You back up drives D and E locally on the public server late in the evening.
- You archive the Wednesday backup. The remaining days you append to tapes.
- You always select **Verify After Backup** and the **Full Detail** log option.

On Monday a user tells you that the following three files are corrupt, and the user is not sure if changes were made on Thursday or Friday.

- D:\Library\Templates\Timesheet.doc
- D:\Data\Accounting\AR.mdb
- D:\Data\Sales\Pricelist.xls

You do the following:

1. Check your backup schedule, which is as follows.

Monday	Tuesday	Wednesday	Thursday	Friday
I 1	I 2	N 3	I 4	I 5
I 1	I 2	N 6	I 4	I 5

N = Normal   I = Incremental

From this schedule, can you determine the last time the files were backed up?

____

2. From Windows NT Explorer, open D:\Labfiles\Backup.log.
3. Search for the corrupted files.

When was the last time they were backed up?

____

On what tape will you find the files that you need?

____

Exercise 2
Creating and Adding a User to the Restore Operators Group

In this exercise, you will create a local group called Restore Operators and grant the group the **Restore files and directories** user right. You will then give a user the rights to restore the computer by adding his or her account to a global group and assigning the global group membership in the Restore Operators group.

Note Complete the following procedure from the BDC only.

➤ **To create a Restore Operators group**

1. Start User Manager for Domains.
2. Create a local group named Restore Operators.
3. On the **Policies** menu, click **User Rights**.

   The **User Rights Policy** dialog box appears.
4. Grant the following user rights to the Restore Operators group:
   - **Log on locally**
   - **Restore files and directories**
   - **Shut down the system**
5. Click **OK** to apply your changes.
6. Create a global group named Restore Only.
7. Add the Restore Only group to the Restore Operators group.

➤ **To give a user the rights to restore to the computer**

Note Complete the following from both computers.

---

1. Create a user account and add it to the Restore Only group.
2. Close User Manager for Domains.
3. From a command prompt, type **net accounts /sync** and press ENTER to make the account available throughout the domain immediately.

Exercise 3
Restoring a File from Tape

In this exercise, you will use the Backup Simulation program to restore files from tape based on specific criteria. This simulation will include:

- Finding a file in the Backup Log.
- Selecting a backup set and creating a catalog.
- Selecting a file to restore.
- Selecting the restore and log options.

The following are the criteria to follow for this exercise:

- Restore the file Sven.doc.
- Verify the restore.
- Restore the file to its source directory.
- Restore file permissions.
- Log full details of the restore.

Note The Backup Simulation program allows you to perform a restore without having a tape drive connected to your computer.

➤ **To find the file to restore in the Backup Log**

1. In Windows NT Explorer, open D:\Winnt\Backup.log.
2. Find the Backup Log and open it.
3. Search the Backup Log for the file Sven.doc.

   Write the path for the document.

   ____

4. Close the Backup Log.

➤ To restore files from tape

1. Click **Backup Simulation** on the taskbar to restore the application.
2. Verify that the Tapes window is the active window.

   What type of backup set was used to back up the data?

   ____

3. In the right pane of the Tapes window, double-click the backup set to load the backup set catalog.

   Note The Backup Simulation creates only one backup set. As a result, you only need to load a backup set catalog.

   The *tape_name* window appears. Notice that the catalog status information appears under **Summary**.

4. When the cataloging operation is finished, click **OK**.

   The backup set contents are displayed in the *tape_name* window.

5. Expand the folder hierarchy to locate the file that you want.
6. Select the check box of the file that you want to restore, and then click **Restore**.

   The **Restore Information** dialog box appears.

   Who owns the tape?

   ____

7. In the **Restore to Drive** box, type **d:** and verify that the **Alternative Path** box is empty.
8. Click **Verify After Restore** and **Restore File Permissions**, and then click **Full Detail**.
9. Click **OK**.

   The **Restore Status** window appears, and then the **Verify Status** window appears.

   What restore operations does Windows NT Backup verify?

   ____

10. When the restore is finished, the following message appears under **Summary**:

    ```
    "The operation was successful"
    ```

11. Click **OK**.
12. Exit the Backup Simulation program.